To the draftee,
the guy who does
the fighting.

Who Will Do Our Fighting for Us?

by
George E. Reedy

Introduction by
Edward M. Kennedy

The World Publishing Company
New York and Cleveland

Published by The World Publishing Company
2231 West 110th Street, Cleveland, Ohio 44102

Published simultaneously in Canada
by Nelson, Foster & Scott Ltd.

First Printing—1969

Library of Congress Catalog Card Number: 78–85934
Printed in the United States of America

WORLD PUBLISHING
TIMES MIRROR

Contents

Introduction

Today's draft law produces many gross inequities, creating unfairness for some of our young men and uncertainty in the lives of others. It operates today unevenly, unfairly, and unpredictably. It was a law designed nearly thirty years ago for other situations, and it is an outdated patchwork of that law and piecemeal amendments. It should be changed, and changed now; there is little excuse for waiting one or two years or more.

Anyone seriously interested in confronting the problems our Selective Service system raises should read carefully George Reedy's *Who Will Do Our Fighting for Us?*, which is an in-depth treatment of many of the draft's most vexing problems.

When we rely upon a system of compulsion to provide manpower for our armed forces, we should be scrupulous to guarantee that the system operates as fairly and equitably as possible. If the system does not, then we are abridging personal freedoms unnecessarily—and this directly contravenes one of the founding principles of our democratic society.

This year alone, about a quarter of a million young men will be involuntarily inducted into the military services. For many of these young men, participation in war violates their deepest moral convictions. Many students turn in their draft deferments, thus rejecting easy avoidance of military service, and challenge their draft status on grounds of conscience—a much more difficult route. Therefore, as Mr. Reedy does, we must look at the difficult question of conscientious objection if we are to understand the controversy surrounding the draft which so deeply disturbs our young people.

Congress has extended the right to claim conscientious objector status to all men who "by religious training and belief" are conscientiously opposed to all forms of war. Those belonging to no orthodox church have, in recent years, had their moral beliefs honored. In 1965, the Supreme Court reinforced this doctrine, holding in the *Seeger* case that a man could be a conscientious objector even if he did not believe in God, so long as his pacifism was backed by deeply felt "religious beliefs." This interpretation was reversed in the 1967 draft law. In my view, this act was not only unwise but, as I pointed out in a Senate speech in February of 1969, of dubious constitutionality as well. An individual whose life pattern indicates his moral opposition to all war should not be forced to violate his conscience because he does not believe in an orthodox God.

I agree with Mr. Reedy's conclusion and that of the single most thorough public study of the draft—the National Advisory Commission on Selective Service, chaired by former Assistant Attorney General Burke Marshall, on which George Reedy served—that "the nation must now, and in the foreseeable future, have a system which includes the draft." This is simply because our first concern must be for guaranteeing a continuing supply of manpower for national defense purposes, and past experience has amply demonstrated that the draft provides just such a guarantee.

But while we preserve the draft in force and effort, we must correct its present defects and work toward these three goals in the draft laws: *flexibility*—the potential to adjust to high or low manpower needs; *certainty*—a concern for uniformity and for predictability so that every young man will know to as great an extent as possible at any time if and when he might be called to duty; and *fairness*—an ever-present regard for equal treatment for every young man in every population group. To reach these goals, the reforms must focus on two elements, as George Reedy proposes: first, drafting the youngest first, at age nineteen; and second, drastically curtailing deferments, with the choice for service made by random selection.

In this eloquent essay, Mr. Reedy clearly defines the many defects in the present draft law. He also directly confronts the proponents of a volunteer army by illustrating the strong possibility that the raising of such a military force might magnify the present economic inequality in the draft —that our soldiers would come from the lower economic classes, and might well form a largely black army. This would serve only to increase the separatism between the military and civilian sectors of our society.

In the discussions of draft reform, we must be careful to keep in clear focus an accurate picture of precisely what it is which is under discussion. Much is currently being made, for example, of the concept of a volunteer army. But what, in fact, those who urge the United States to move to this position are saying is that we move to a *professional* armed force—an armed force not based on a continual turnover of civilians, but an armed force based entirely on men who will make the army their career.

At present, nearly 70 percent of our armed forces are volunteers, and the remaining 30 percent are draftees. Nearly all the Air Force, Navy, and Marines are volunteers. The best estimates we have available indicate that after Vietnam, when our armed forces return to a 2.5 million force level from their present 3.5 million force level, our necessary manpower needs may well be filled by voluntary enlistments. But this will not really be a professional army, because there will continue to be high levels of turnover from short-term enlistments. What we may well have after Vietnam is a situation exactly like today's—except that while the draft will exist, it will not actually be used to produce draftees for the military. What it will do, on the other hand, is to provide us with the back-up flexibility we need to meet any contingency.

Were we to move to a professional army, as opposed to an army whose members were largely voluntary enlistees, we would have to face a number of very difficult questions. We simply do not have these answers at this time. For example, we do not have an accurate idea of what a professional army would cost. Estimates have ranged from an additional $4 billion to $17 billion a year. Furthermore, we do not know whether it would be a black army. Nor do we know what the impact would be of a growing separatism between the civilian and the military.

For these and other reasons, I have for some years urged the creation of a blue-ribbon, independent group to try as best they can to answer these questions. President Nixon in March of this year indicated that he had appointed just such a group, and I am confident that when the group makes its report, we shall for the first time have the information we all need before we can judge the wisdom of moving to a professional army.

Mr. Reedy discusses other troublesome questions of draft reform, and he does so from the vantage point of one who served on the Marshall Commission, and who has subsequently devoted much time to examining the issues in some detail. His thoughtful treatment of these issues helps greatly to bring us closer to an understanding of how we must treat this matter which so vitally touches the lives of our young men and women.

Edward M. Kennedy
May, 1969

Foreword

This essay is very distinctly not a labor of love. It reaches conclusions which are unpleasant and expresses opinions which are strongly reminiscent of a piece of hard chalk squealing down a blackboard. It has only one virtue. It comes from thoughts which have been formed out of the personal experience of two generations.

I was a draftee; my father was a "volunteer" soldier. Perhaps the contrast is what has led to my present position. I am old enough to have heard from past generations of what professional soldiering really amounted to. I am young enough to have served as a conscript in a major war. Neither experience appeals to me as an adequate way of life. But I cannot wish them both out of existence as a means of conducting human affairs. I recognize them as reactions to problems which must, somehow, be answered.

In the early part of this century, it was common for young Irish boys to run away from home in their early teens, lie about their ages, and join the army. My father was one of those boys. He left his home in Marquette, Michigan, when he was thirteen years old. That was too young to enter the army even in those days and he knocked around the country for two years, joining the cavalry in St. Louis when he was fifteen years old. Recruiting sergeants were not very particular about birth certificates (which my father didn't have anyway because they weren't issued in the lumber camp where he was born) and didn't check very hard for parental consent. One year later, he was a combat veteran, stumping down the street on his wooden leg with $30 put into his pocket every month by a government grateful for his defense of King's Ranch against the forces of Pancho Villa.

Dad never complained about his military service or what happened to him. No matter how he looked at it, it was better than topping timber at 20 degrees below zero in northern Michigan. He did, at times, comment bitterly upon the bleakness of life where he had been born and upon the impossibility of an ambitious young man finding an existence of fulfillment. Dad was not a philosopher or a historian and it never occurred to him that he was descended from a people who had made their living for centuries largely by the export of their youth to professional armies in other lands. And he was not alone in his experience. Years later, he showed my

12

mother a picture of him swimming in the Rio Grande with other cavalry troopers. My mother gasped. Alongside him was her cousin, Tom Mulvaney. He, too, had run away from home in his early teens and joined the army. It was better than rolling steel in a grimy mill town in southern Indiana.

As for myself, I first encountered the "Military Manpower Problem" as a young reporter covering the Burke-Wadsworth bill (the precursor of the present draft act) in 1940. I wrote stories on its passage up to the point of Presidential signature, and shortly thereafter I stood in the Labor Department Auditorium while Franklin D. Roosevelt, a blindfold over his eyes, drew the first number from the famous goldfish bowl. Eventually, my own number came up and I was one of those who received a Greeting from the President informing me of a decision that had been taken by a board composed of my friends and neighbors.

The war did not end my close contact with military manpower problems. In 1951, I found myself, as a staff member of the Senate Preparedness Subcommittee, attempting to secure Congressional approval of Universal Military Training—an effort that fell short by only a few votes. And in 1966, the President placed me on the Burke Marshall Commission (the National Advisory Commission on Selective Service), which conducted what is probably the most comprehensive study of Selective Service by an outside group in modern times.

During the course of my lifetime, I have formed

some strong personal convictions on this subject. They are not convictions that I necessarily like. But they are firmly held. I do not relish either a conscript or a "volunteer" army. But I believe that a democracy can live more easily with the conscripts than it can with the professionals. The former do not like what they are doing—*and that is precisely the reason why they should be preferred.*

A conscript army, as long as it is drafted under rules which assure representation of the whole population, is one which must be led, not ordered. It cannot hold together indefinitely unless there is some popular consensus behind it. The risks are shared by all—and this means that the political leaders must take into account the popular will when they order their troops into battle. They can move against reluctance on the part of large segments of the population; but they must have a large share of acquiescence before they order the fighting. *And when they do move into battle, they must hold the feet of the whole nation to the fire.* Under Selective Service, they cannot count upon the passive support of constituents on the grounds that the constituents are not disturbed in their everyday lives.

This does not mean, of course, that only "good" wars will be fought with conscripts and only "bad" wars with professionals. But it does mean that the consequences of *any* war will be brought home to every citizen if it is fought with draftees. And there is no other safeguard of freedom. If we all share in the burdens, we are all

14

likely to be more particular in how those burdens are incurred.

Selective Service is, in my judgment, the only manner in which we can assure the sharing of the burdens. In the late twentieth century, with its highly developed technology and its interdependent economy, there is no other method of raising a citizens' army. The alternative is to rely upon mercenaries who are expensive and who do *not* exert upon their government any of the pressures that are essential if political leaders are to be responsive to their people.

The present system of conscription is woefully inadequate for our society and for our problems. It must be altered fundamentally and I welcome the efforts to do so that are being made in many quarters, such as Senator Edward Kennedy's present bill. My concern is that these efforts may be lost unless we have a clear picture of the real alternatives that confront our society.

If this essay does nothing else, I hope it helps to focus attention on some of the real issues. They do not cluster around the inconveniences and the perils that may be caused to some of our people. They do center around the problem of how a workable structure can be erected to preserve democracy. If we start thinking in those terms, there is hope for the future.

1

The Context of the Debate

Walking through a vine-covered archway on the campus of one of America's oldest and most respected universities, the eager, bespectacled youth leader was explaining to me his concept of how the "voluntary army" would work: "I think of it as a twentieth-century version of grabbing a musket from the wall in the middle of the night and rushing to the city gates to defend my home from an attacker," he said.

The sheer puerility of this idea became apparent to him after a few, tactful questions. Even he conceded that very few Americans could keep an F-111 or a light tank on the front lawn available for a midnight dash to the Arctic DEW line or a paratroop landing ground. "But I still keep hoping that we can turn this business over to somebody who wants to do it," he said wistfully. Then, with a burst of candor, he added: "Maybe it's true that I am for the volunteer army because I want somebody else to do the volunteering."

The young man was not as sophisticated in the intricate issues of military manpower as the orator who, later in the day, lectured some 500 students on "Alternatives to Selective Service." The speaker avoided the obvious intellectual trap of the "musket from the wall" and the dash to the city gates. But the arguments were basically in tune with the proposals of the youth leader—lacking only the honest recognition of the real issue.

There is perhaps no other national issue of such continuing, high visibility as Selective Service. It has been the law of the land almost continuously since 1940 and has figured in every major war this nation has fought since 1860. It has been studied and restudied by military experts, Congressional committees, groups of private citizens, and one Presidential Commission. Literally millions of men have received the traditional Greetings from the President informing them of a decision by a group of their neighbors, and it has been a Damoclean sword hanging over American youth since the outbreak of the Korean War.

Normally, the issues involved in any factor so close to our daily lives are reasonably well understood, if not by the public generally at least by its more articulate leaders. There may be disagreement—even heated disagreement—over any question that agitates human beings. But as a general rule, the context of the argument is clear and the divisions involve differing philosophical reactions to alternative courses.

18

It cannot truthfully be said that this state of affairs describes the public debate on Selective Service. There is probably no other subject which provokes such bitter disputes over options that are not available and conditions that do not exist. The young man who thought of the military manpower problem in terms of defending a frontier outpost against marauding Indians is in good company. His exposition of the question was on the same level as most of the national dialogue and considerably more colorful.

The passage of time does not seem to improve the quality of the discussion. In this area, at least, we do not learn from the past. Many of the arguments that are advanced today do not vary in the least from those that I learned as a young reporter covering the enactment of the Burke-Wadsworth bill (the progenitor of the present law) in 1940. A modern-day advocate of the voluntary army could use, with only minor changes, Senate speeches made by Ernest Lundeen in 1940, and draft-card burners could repeat, virtually intact, the testimony given by members of the War Resisters League before the Senate Military Affairs Committee earlier in the same year.

The fact that the arguments vary so little is of basic significance. The world context in which any military matter must be discussed has changed tremendously since 1940. Selective Service, for all its crucial importance to the individual, is obviously an issue inextricably intertwined with the nation's diplomatic and military

19

policies, and if the dialogue within such a setting remains unaltered over a span of twenty-nine years, the only reasonable conclusion is that it must be marked by an air of unreality.

A note of caution is necessary at this point in order to put the discussion into proper perspective. The *workings* of Selective Service are quite well understood by large segments of our population. Many college students can discuss the fine points of draft procedure with the precision of a maritime lawyer arguing a salvage case, and they have an incredibly exact knowledge of the prejudices and propensities of any draft board which might affect their lives. They can outline the appeals system; differentiate between exemption and other deferment categories and forecast to the percentage point the number of student deferments that will be granted in any area in which they are interested. On this subject, virtually all of them are straight A students. (It should be added that noncollege youth do not have this same knowledge and frequently are drafted when alternate procedures are open to them. This is not a question of intelligence but rests upon the fact that they do not live in communities where the subject is a matter of continuing discussion.)

This minute knowledge of procedures, however, rarely extends to the context of the law itself, and in this respect campus discussions are markedly similar to those in any other forum. The college student has an individual advantage over less fortunate members of his generation not only because as an undergraduate he is entitled to a deferment but because he is quite likely to "know his rights." When it comes to avoiding the draft, knowledge is power, and it is apparent to anyone who has spent any time with young people recently that there is absolutely no stigma attached to the use of that power. The age of the "White Feather" is dead (and I wonder how many of my younger readers will even know what I am talking about).

It can be said with equal validity, however, that when it comes to *changing* the draft knowledge is also power —but it is knowledge of a different order and here the college student is generally as deficient as anyone else. To him, Selective Service is, understandably, an intensely personal matter, and he is as oblivious to the larger policy issues as are his elders when *they* discuss the youthful revolt against a society and against policies which are subject to valid criticism.

There is a general rule of human conduct which should be borne in mind by all who seek to change social institutions. It is that unyielding insistence upon impossible goals results in the sacrifice of possible goals, no matter how desirable the latter may be. If this precept is to be considered a factor in solving any political equation, of course, it calls for an extraordinary exercise of human judgment in differentiating the possible from the impossible. Under any circumstances, the resultant mental fatigue is considerable and even a limited success is possible only upon the basis of knowledge. But it is a salutary exercise, as worthy causes often founder on the unrealistic aims of their leaders—not on the devilish machinations of their opponents.

This principle applies with great force to the whole discussion of Selective Service. As an institution, it has successfully resisted major changes for twenty-nine years—even under circumstances where major changes were obviously needed. It has beaten back advocates of Universal Military Training (which is quite a different thing) and it has withstood all efforts to reintroduce pure voluntarism. The alterations that were *absolutely necessary* have originated within the system itself, and very few innovations from the outside have had the serious consideration of Congress.

The power of the hierarchy which controls Selective Service rests upon a very simple and obvious base. *The members know what they are doing.* They understand the nit-picking details and the broad implications. They have ability and they know how to use it. They have lived with the subject for more than three decades (General Hershey was studying the field long before the 1940 law was enacted) and they know all the answers. Finally, they have established working relationships with Congress and with state governments that are based upon the strongest of all human bonds—the sure knowledge that they can perform that which they promise to perform.

Of all the myths I have encountered on college campuses, the most absurd is the idea that Lewis B. Hershey is a second-rate time server who owes his position solely to friendships he has established over the years with senile Congressional committee chairmen. This concept, of course, has survived very few campus appearances by Hershey. His steel-trap mind, card-file memory, and comprehensive grasp of the subject are just too obvious to permit the audience to sustain its illusions. And to finish off the picture, generations of critics have gone through his agency with a fine-tooth comb to locate evidence of chicanery and have emerged empty-handed.

This combination of qualities makes Hershey a formidable opponent in any debate. And when he is wrong —as this writer believes him to be wrong on many issues—the consequences can be tragic. There simply is not enough knowledge available and concentrated on a continuing basis to best him in an argument.

As an example, the Burke Marshall Commission, composed of some of America's most influential citizens, accumulated enough knowledge in the course of a two-year study to mount serious challenges to some of General Hershey's most cherished concepts. The recommendations, made to the President, were transmitted to Congress and studied by two Congressional committees and another advisory commission established by one of those committees. But despite the impressive credentials of the sponsors (who included leading educators, businessmen, lawyers, a distinguished retired Marine Corps General, and a respected former Assistant Secretary of Defense for Manpower) the proposals for change didn't have a chance. The members of the Commission disbanded the day they completed their report. Members of Congress were well aware that they would never see most of them again. But Hershey would be there; Hershey would be on the scene; Hershey would be dealing with them on a day-to-day basis. The outcome was inevitable. The report was received politely and treated with respect; General Hershey was received enthusiastically and treated with adulation. There were a few minor changes and life went on as before.

The few minor changes, however, had consequences —not so much on the draftees as on the Selective Service system itself. Within two years, it became apparent that a supposedly closed issue had to be reopened. At the time that this is being written (February, 1969), there is a prospect that the Congress will reconsider the law and at least make some substantial amendments.

What will happen, of course, depends upon the manner in which the debate is handled—the reason for this discussion. It is the view of this writer that it is highly unlikely that the draft will be abolished in the foreseeable future—or at least in time to affect the lives of those who now stand in the shadow of military service. But it is quite possible to make important improvements in the sense of reducing the inequities, introducing a higher degree of effectiveness, and increasing public confidence in its operation.

The improvements cannot be made if the strength of the arguments available to those who resist change

24

is underestimated. Nor will it help to misjudge their competency or their character. And many high expectations will be cruelly dashed if the legislative process begins with unrealistic concepts of what can be done.

The political impact of Selective Service is worthy of a discussion all by itself. The arguments cannot be quieted by a restatement of the law or by promises of future action. This is because those who are disturbed are not really dissenting against the draft but against being drafted to fight in a war which they consider irrelevant to their lives. This distinction may seem academic but a little reflection will make it clear that the difference is vital.

This nation has lived with the Selective Service Act since 1940. There have been changes and modifications, and draft calls have gone up and draft calls have gone down—even to the point of nonexistence. During most of that period, however (there were fifteen months in 1947 and 1948 when the draft was suspended totally and the system placed on stand-by), the machinery has been in operation and young men have been classified and made subject to call. The only public clamor for revision has risen during unpopular wars, and it is a safe prediction that an end to the Vietnamese conflict tomorrow night would coincide with an end to any massive draft dissent, provided the cessation of hostilities were followed by a period of peace and a shrinkage in military manpower requirements.

This, of course, should not be construed as an argument against dissent or against revision. The motivation for protest is frequently irrelevant to the merits of the protest, and points are not answered by impugning the good faith of those who make them. In the judgment of this writer there are both valid and invalid criticisms of Selective Service, and the fact that very few criticized the system during the years of relative peace has nothing to do with whether action should be taken now. But it does have something to do with the conduct of those who are in a position of responsibility and must sustain the confidence of the people in their government.

A promise to end the draft and go to a "voluntary" system at the end of the Vietnamese war will have absolutely no effect on the college campuses of the nation. This is the "now" generation and it feels no more "nower" in any other field than it does in this one. The college debates are not addressed to problems of military manpower policy—long range or short range. Students couldn't care less and, with a few exceptions, they are perfectly willing to leave such details to experts —as long as those experts leave them alone.

Students are refreshingly candid about this attitude and make no effort to pretend otherwise. Those who have really deep feelings about Vietnam and Selective Service as an institution are relatively few and draw their support largely from others who simply state they don't want to be drafted. As one said to me at Brandeis University: "If somebody else wants to fight this war, it's O.K. with me. I just don't feel that this war has anything to do with me and that I should be asked to fight it."

This particular student expressed himself somewhat better than others and was a little less free with fog language. But anyone who believes that he was not expressing a widespread attitude simply has not spent much time on college campuses.

The expressions vary. A farm boy in a junior college in upstate New York asked: "Isn't it true that your chances of being drafted depend on who you know, not what you know?" A bearded Negro with a necklace dangling on his chest said: "Man, I got news for you. I ain't going." A business major in a conservative, Catholic, Middle-Western school said: "Of course, I'll go if they catch up to me but they are going to have to run like hell and after they get me, they won't like it."

Naturally, these are all individual expressions. What is impressive is that they were made in the midst of large groups of students and accepted as a matter of community consensus—not as an exercise in provocation. It is just taken for granted that every male is planning draft avoidance as carefully as he is planning his career.

These thoughts are advanced here only as a caution against political promises that cannot be carried out. Sometimes a promise is enough to assure the loyalty of a following. But a promise for action down the road in this instance is not enough. Any promise in this area must be kept and kept immediately or college youth will take their political business elsewhere—more likely to those who made no promises at all.

This is a dangerous area for promises—even implied promises. The future of Selective Service is tied to many factors beyond the control of America's leaders and no one can predict its future development with confidence. Furthermore, at this stage it is not a political issue in the sense of a program which we can have or not have in accordance with our desires. We committed ourselves to compulsory military service twenty-nine years ago as a tool which must be used under some circumstances and which might be suspended temporarily under others. As a tool, it is subject to improvement and the effects of its use depend upon the judiciousness of those who wield it. But after twenty-nine years, it has become a basic element in our national policy and responsible consideration of so-called alternatives demands an assessment of the conditions and the other elements of policy to which it is related.

The possibility of going to a "voluntary" system, for example, depends upon the demands of the international situation. This is a truism which, however obvious, intrudes very little into public discussion, which seems to take for granted that foreign-affairs problems will vanish after the fighting is over in Vietnam. But who can predict international developments for the next year, let alone the next five years, which would be a reasonable time span to serve as an assumption for determining military manpower policy?

This writer believes that there is good reason to be skeptical about a purely "voluntary" military system under any circumstances. The basis for the skepticism will be explored later in this book. But there is no need to take that leap for the moment. The first task is to examine the situation in which we now find ourselves and to determine which alternatives are truly practical. It may well be that they are fewer than we think and that our political and ideological energies could well be channeled in other directions.

2
The Principle of Uncertainty

In many years of individual and group discussions, this writer has yet to meet an aggressive advocate of the voluntary army who is a potential volunteer or an aggressive advocate of Selective Service who is in danger of being drafted.

This factor casts a peculiar coloration over the national debate. There are many issues which can be settled by invoking the judgment of impartial people who have no personal bias whatsoever. In this area we are denied that comforting expedient. We have no alternative other than to face the issue squarely, trying to discount our own predilections in an effort to attain objectivity.

It is a tribute to the common sense of the American people that we have done as well as we have in the field of military manpower policy. No one can pretend that we have fought any war with an "ideal" system.

But we have managed, on every occasion, to recruit the men that we need—frequently under heavy protest but without smashing our basic social structure.

In most of our wars, however, we have had time to improvise recruitment policies after the outbreak of actual hostilities. Even in World War II, where civilization was introduced to the concept of the national blitzkrieg, England bought for us sufficient breathing space to develop a modern army. Unfortunately, we can no longer count on the luxury of even a few months to arm, equip, and train our warriors once we know they will be needed. In the modern world, the outcome of any military operation depends upon the preparations that were made in periods of relative peace and quiet.

The most cursory reflection makes it quite clear that our preparation for the past two wars was not very good. Korea was a conflict fought to a great extent by reservists from World War II—thus placing men in double jeopardy. Vietnam has generated unrest and discontent to a point where it toppled an administration that had entered office four years earlier with the largest popular majority in our entire history.

It would be a major error to attribute the unpopularity of these two wars solely to the military manpower policies which were followed. But there can be no doubt that the tragic inequality of sacrifice which characterized both struggles was a major factor in bringing public opinion to the boiling point. Korea was a dreary account of men who had to leave promising careers and

32

face an enemy for the second time in their lives; Vietnam has been—and continues to be—a heavy imbalance of burdens upon some of the young people of our country.

In each instance, we were operating under a system which had been established to meet the recruitment problems of a different war in a different era. We plunged into both conflicts with a Selective Service law that had been devised substantially for World War II. We have made very few changes to this date which reflect the changed situation.

The basic assumption of the current law is that war requires the total mobilization of the resources of the nation. Under these circumstances, the problem of equality of sacrifice is of secondary concern. The major need is for adequate authority to allocate manpower so it can be employed most effectively. If everyone is contributing to the war effort, under a system where the determination of who will do what has been made by a national authority, there is no question of equity.

The Selective Service law does not, of course, grant the government authority to order people to work in specified private industries. But the same purpose is accomplished by establishing categories of work for which able-bodied men can be exempted from compulsory military service. In a situation of total mobilization, everyone has a clear conscience. If a healthy man is not in uniform, it can be concluded with reasonable certainty that he is making his contribution to national survival in his civilian job.

In a war whose objective is total victory, these assumptions are tenable even though they do not quite match the reality. In World War II we may even have overmobilized. But no one was disturbed. The national desire to defeat the Axis powers was so overwhelming that Americans were clamoring for even stronger blows than were dealt or that needed to be dealt. Virtually every American wanted to see Hitler, Mussolini, and Tojo beaten to their knees.

Korea and Vietnam, however, were not military operations launched for securing a clear-cut victory over an enemy. In each case, the goal was simply to enforce recognition of an international status quo and to *avoid* the type of confrontation which could be ended only by the complete defeat of an adversary. Therefore, military commanders in the field had to spend almost as much time calculating what they could *not* do as what they could do and, in global terms, hostilities were confined to relatively small areas.

Whether such limited wars are viable instruments of national policy is a disputed question which requires more examination than can be given here. But there can be no doubt whatsoever that they create a new set of conditions and consequently a new set of military recruitment problems. Of these, the most important is a negative factor. *They simply do not call for total mobilization. And the inescapable consequence is that if they*

34

are to be fought, there must be inequality of sacrifice.
Any effort to give all Americans the feeling that they
are sharing the burden must, in the very nature of the
situation, be patently artificial.

The avowed objective of limited war is to "contain"
the Communist world on the thesis that its expansionist
tendencies eventually will cool off if frustrated. The
burden of fighting limited engagements is held—quite
properly—to be far preferable to the nuclear holocaust
that would result from a big-power war.

There is persuasive logic to this concept and few
people will argue against it as long as it is stated in general and not specific terms. No one welcomes nuclear
destruction nor are many Americans willing to sacrifice
freedom to Communist aggression. The limited war appears to be a course "in the middle of the road"—the
position which accords with the pragmatic instincts of
Americans generally. It avoids obliteration and it avoids
surrender while leaving open the possibility of a "deal"
which will settle the divisions in the world through
rational discussion.

It is also a strategy, however, which requires the
United States to maintain a strong, mobile striking force
which can be expanded with little effort. The expansion
factor is crucial because the inherent nature of the
problem is such that no one can forecast with any confidence the future requirements of the military establishment. The best that can be done is to make a minimum estimate of the force that will be needed and

35

establish the machinery that can add to it rapidly.

It is tempting, of course, to seek out rationalizations for holding down the basic defensive force and for failing to set up the necessary expansion machinery which, no matter how well handled, is bound to be unpleasant. This tendency has led to fantastic pontification concerning military strategy on the part of otherwise sensible people. Unfortunately, there have been occasions when the pontification has been substituted for national policy, and the consequences have been unfortunate.

The development of the atomic bomb during World War II fostered, among other things, an illusion that humanity had entered an age of push-button warfare. In this era, it was held, the man with the rifle was obsolete and the nation's military establishment would be manned by physicists, chemists, engineers—and a few lowly technicians to replace blown-out vacuum tubes. The infantryman would be out of place and useful only for ceremonial guard duty.

This particular illusion vanished with the outbreak of hostilities in Korea. Our government did not want to concede the Communists a quick and easy victory in the occupation of South Korea; but it did not seem very wise to risk a major war with the Communist bloc by resorting to the only implements of "push-button" war that really existed—our atomic arsenal and its delivery systems. Therefore, the United States turned to the only available course—hastily throwing in whatever reserves could be scraped together and drafting men at a frantic rate.

Frantic is the only word that accurately describes what happened. There had been no draft calls whatsoever during the seven months that preceded the August, 1950, invasion of South Korea and only a tiny trickle of inductions (inductions usually lag behind calls). In September, the call was 50,000—all for the army—and by November the call was 70,000. Furthermore, there was virtually no lag between call and induction. Call, notice, and induction were accomplished in a matter of days.

Strangely, the illusion reappeared very shortly after the Korean cease-fire, although this time in a presentation of greater plausibility. It was given the name "massive retaliation" by the late Secretary of State John Foster Dulles and assumed that the United States would define certain areas of national interest and would strike back with its nuclear power if those areas were transgressed. Under this doctrine, the military eggs were placed in the atomic basket and when President Eisenhower decided to land foot soldiers in Lebanon to forestall a threatened Communist takeover, we found our tactical airlift resources were under heavy stress.

Right now, there is no serious contention in the national dialogue that push buttons and atomic bombs and missiles are adequate for the foreign policy of the United States. It is generally recognized that the atomic

37

age lends itself at best to a balance of terror and that sole reliance upon fissionable material for our defense is merely a reliance upon mutual self-destruction. Humanity has not yet advanced to the point of renouncing slaughter as an instrument of international relations; but it does have an antipathy to universal obliteration.

The impulse to indulge in sweeping generalizations that justify abandonment of Selective Service, however, remains as strong as ever. In the current debate, it has settled upon guerrilla warfare of the Vietnam variety as a factor which requires a different response than conventional land fighting. The philosophical implications were drawn by President Nixon in a radio address while he was still a candidate for the White House.

Richard Nixon told his audience that in the nuclear age "huge ground armies operating in massive formations would be terribly vulnerable." As far as an "all-out non-nuclear war" is concerned, he continued, it "is hard to see it happening again." He then turned to guerrilla war in Vietnam and said: "Here we need a highly professional, highly motivated force of men trained in the techniques of counterinsurgency. Vietnam has shown us that success in such wars may depend on whether our soldiers are linguists and civil-affairs specialists, as well as warriors. Also, the complex weapons of modern war demand a higher level of technical and professional skill."

He added, of course, that this country will still need "conventional" forces but not "in such quantity that we cannot meet our manpower needs through voluntary enlistments."

There is no reason to question the sincerity of Mr. Nixon's analysis. Any dissent expressed here is intended with all due respect. But somehow, a conclusion that we do *not* have to do something (in this instance, operate a Selective Service system) because of the nature of modern warfare is hardly reassuring. It is even less reassuring when Mr. Nixon tells us that we cannot change the system as long as we are in Vietnam.

The question arises automatically: If we must have Selective Service for Vietnam, what are we going to do if we get into another—and similar—war in the near future?

Of course, Mr. Nixon does not intend to get into such a war. But neither did his predecessors. Human will is not the only determining factor in history—especially individual human will. And whether we should or should not have plunged into Vietnam is one thing; whether we should have the strength to meet such a contingency generally is still another.

The unfortunate and obvious truth is that only a deliberate aggressor can predict with any degree of accuracy whether there will be a war and how it will be fought. The party that forces the issue determines both the when and the how. And whatever doubts many Americans may have as to the wisdom of many of our policies, it takes genuine distortion of the facts and long leaps of fancy to portray the United States as a deliberate aggressor. There is no reason to believe that it will move to this stage under Mr. Nixon.

This discussion has been intended to set some sort of a background against which the issue of the draft can be discussed with some perspective. The discussion was necessary because, all too often, the question has been discussed as though there were no context whatsoever. It is far too easily forgotten that Selective Service evolved as an institution to meet specific needs. It is not sacrosanct any more than any other institution, but a responsible approach to changing it requires either the provision of new methods for meeting the needs or a reasonably satisfactory demonstration that they no longer exist or were exaggerated originally.

It can be taken as a truism that no military manpower system will be adequate unless it is based upon a clear picture of the world situation. And the keynote of this era is uncertainty. Perhaps the real tragedy of this generation is that it cannot even be certain about doom. It is not that the outlook is bleak. It is that we simply don't know what is going to happen from one day to the next.

Any school child can put his finger on a dozen spots on the globe where trouble might break out tomorrow morning. And if, by some miracle, there is no crisis in any one of them overnight, he can probably find twelve new spots the next morning. It is a volatile age—one in which long-neglected problems are suddenly rising to the surface and demanding action.

We are not, of course, completely helpless to make judgments about the world situation. It is no longer likely—though not impossible—that we will be surprised by the introduction of totally new weapons or totally new methods of fighting. This state of affairs arises less from an increase in the cloak-and-dagger type of spy than from the fact that the new weapons grow out of a technology which has become so great in size that even a society which is intended to be closed cannot achieve industrial invisibility.

Our judgments, however, have a reasonable degree of validity only in the field of capability; when it comes to reading intentions we can only guess. We know, for example, that the Soviet Union, through its mastery of East Germany, has the *capacity* to deny peaceful access to Berlin. But we do not know that they will exercise this capability *at any given time* and we cannot even rely upon Communist statements that they will or will not do so. Even more important, when a Berlin blockade looms as a threat, we can only speculate as to the level of response that will be required to avert such action.

This is the factor that has more to do with our military manpower policies than anything else—the factor of uncertainty. We live in a world where we do not know what tomorrow will bring—but we do know that we can awaken any morning and find ourselves plunged into catastrophic events where the likelihood of our survival as a free nation is contingent upon the speed of our reactions. And we have learned through bitter experience that we cannot rely upon modern science and technology to substitute for muscle and blood. The business of slaughter still takes men.

The absolute pacifist, who believes in a categorical imperative that forbids him to kill his fellow man under any circumstances, can dismiss the world context as irrelevant. He can take a stand against any type of military establishment and argue his case with complete logic. His assumptions may be questionable but he need not pick his way through the intricacies of military recruitment because he does not think there should be any at all.

Those who concede the necessity of fighting under some circumstances, however, are compelled, if they wish to be responsible, to take a stand on which military manpower policies they consider effective. They cannot approve—even partially—of war and then ignore the physical problems of fighting a war or of assuring that a nation be ready to fight. In addition, of course, they must face a number of moral issues, but these will be raised in a later chapter since here we are discussing only the general context within which we must debate selective service.

The principle of uncertainty would appear to limit our choices as to what kind of a military establishment we should devise. Logically, only two paths are conceivable. One is to provide and maintain a permanent force sufficiently large to meet every contingency or every combination of contingencies; the other is to devise a flexible system of military responses based on a minimum force capable of shielding us against a total initial defeat, with well-oiled machinery to provide a rapid and effective build-up against emergencies.

The latter path, however imperfect may have been our execution, has marked the course of our military policies for the past two decades. It is likely to continue. Orators may speak in ringing terms of a defense establishment "second to none" and capable of "defeating any adversary." But it is improbable that any person in a position of responsibility will try to saddle this country with the economic and social burden of a permanent force large enough to meet any foe or any combination of foes. Only a totally mobilized nation could do it and not even the Soviet Union is *that* totally mobilized.

A discussion of Selective Service and the volunteer army that omits the question of flexibility is like a discussion of taxation that omits the question of its impact upon our economy. Such a debate, unfortunately, goes on all the time. It is this factor that tends to give much of the public dialogue the flavor of Alice's discussion with the Queen in the croquet garden. Effective new policies are not produced by ignoring the realities upon which older policies were based.

The strength of the Selective Service system is that it meets a basic test. General Hershey has an amazingly effective argument against change which boils down to one sentence. He says: "Whatever else may be said, the Selective Service system has never failed to produce the men that are needed when they are needed." This statement does not have much impact in an oratorical forum or to a young man trying to make decisions about his career. It is a gross oversimplification of the issue. But when it is addressed to men and women who have the responsibility of making decisions on military manpower, it has compelling potency. They are highly unlikely to pay much attention to any argument which avoids the General's point or dismisses it as immaterial.

What this means is that those who seek to change or abolish Selective Service must produce alternatives which are demonstrably superior, or at least equal, in providing the manpower needed by the defense establishment. It is difficult to sustain the contention that this requirement is generally met. The orientation in most forums is directed towards the impact of the system upon the individual, and however legitimate such discussion may be it is hardly likely, by itself, to override the problem of recruitment.

This is why so many pleas for change fall on deaf ears in Congress. It is not that legislators are indifferent to the fate of individuals. It is simply that they are not inclined to grant a fully attentive audience to those who seem to be avoiding the focal point of the problem.

This writer is convinced, both from study and from direct contacts, that no proposals for change which do not take the question of flexibility into account will be very effective with the nation's legislators. This is an effort to explore the implications of that assumption and place the picture into a somewhat clearer perspective. There is no ideal solution to the problem of military recruitment. It is one of those situations, all too frequent in the world, where all we can do is to make the best out of a bad business. We have not made the best out of it yet and perhaps, through some mutual understanding, we can at least reach that stage.

3
The Volunteer Army—Prelude to Disappointment

The generation that yearns for the volunteer army is doomed to become the disappointed generation. The only version it is likely to get is one that will have little effect upon the lives of its members.

This prediction can be made with an unusually high degree of confidence. The odds are heavily in its favor even should Congress approve the administration's volunteer army proposals. These would make some important changes in the nation's military manpower system. But they would *not* meet the demand being pressed so vigorously on college campuses.

The emotional nature of the national debate has obscured the fact that draft-age youth and the administration give totally different meanings to the words "volunteer army." To young people, the phrase means that only those who want to fight will be called upon to do so. To the administration it means that the permanent military establishment will be composed of professional soldiers but that Selective Service will be retained on a "stand-by" basis to draft men in the event of an emergency.

And even should the administration change its definition and accept that of most college youth, it is highly unlikely that Congress would follow its lead. The improbability of either event has been heightened by the Harris Poll, which records a majority of Americans as favoring the present system over volunteering.

Mr. Nixon was perfectly straightforward in the announcement of his intentions when he discussed the volunteer army in October, 1968. His words were plain and are worth quoting verbatim:

In proposing that we start toward ending the draft when the war is over, I would enter two cautions: first, its structure needs to be kept on stand-by in case some all-out emergency requires its reactivation, but this can be done without leaving 20 million young Americans who will come of draft age during the next decade in constant uncertainty and apprehension.

The second caution I would enter is this: the draft can't be ended all at once. It will have to be phased out, so that at every step we can be certain of maintaining our defense strength.

The most interesting aspect of Mr. Nixon's statement is that with this qualification he is proposing to enact the law precisely as it exists right now. The only difference is that he suggests higher pay and better working conditions for America's soldiers—a proposal that is hard to dispute. But the pay increase is of little or no interest to the young people who are demanding a volunteer army. They are asking that those who do not want to fight be relieved of the burden. They are totally indifferent to improvements in the military manpower structure which do not bear upon this point.

Mr. Nixon appears to be proposing something new only because few citizens are aware of the philosophy upon which current law is based. There is a widespread misapprehension that the present system *requires* that men be drafted for the armed services. Nothing could be farther from the actuality.

The laws only provide machinery to draft men when enough cannot be obtained for military needs through voluntary enlistment. If the requirements cannot be met with professionals, then the Selective Service machinery goes into operation. If the requirements can be met, compulsory service is placed on the status of "standby."

In addition to the fifteen-month suspensions in 1947 and 1948 and the seven months of limbo in 1949, there have been a number of occasions when draft calls were either reduced to zero or to a point so low that they were not noticed. No one was called in May or June of 1961 and the monthly calls for the preceding two years were small—never more than 9,000 and in April, 1961, only 1,500. In fiscal 1963, the monthly calls were in the

5,000 to 10,000 range and it was not until fiscal 1966 that they began soaring above 16,000.

There is no legal barrier that prevents the administration from going to a wholly volunteer army tomorrow morning. All that would be required is a directive to the Defense Department to stop issuing manpower calls to the Selective Service system. Congress need not intervene. The only inhibiting factors are the practicalities of the situation.

Of course, Congressional action would be needed to set the pay scales that the administration expects would attract volunteers. But even assuming this legislation is approved, the administration recognizes the need to maintain Selective Service as a "stand-by." They promise the draft will not be used unless the situation requires it, but this is like promising not to ask for a tax increase unless the money is needed.

Even under these circumstances, the practicalities of raising an all-volunteer army are still open to doubt. Forecasts of what it will take to induce men to volunteer are highly questionable. Thus far experience has shown that the major inducement for enlistments is the draft itself.

It is not generally realized that even now most enlistments in the armed services are voluntary rather than compulsory. In 1969, for example, the Defense Department expects to take in 1,050,000 men in both regular and reserve components. But only 260,000 of these will be draftees. The other 790,000 will be "volunteers."

Pentagon manpower experts are realistic about this figure. They divide the volunteers into categories—draft-motivated and other. The draft-motivated people (those who volunteer a step ahead of Selective Service because the act gives them some advantage) come out on top—490,000 compared to 300,000 listed as "other." These statistics apply to a defense establishment of 3,500,000 uniformed men. In a post-Vietnam force, it is assumed that there would be an increase in the percentage of genuine volunteers even without pay increases. But the drafted and draft-motivated categories would still exist, providing 330,000 men out of a total number of 680,000 new recruits.

It is assumed that higher pay scales would attract more recruits and make compulsory service unnecessary. This assumption is backed by a number of studies as to the total cost of pay scales high enough to attract enough volunteers. The estimates range from $4,000,-000,000 to $16,000,000,000 annually. Even if this range is feasible, there is reason to question these figures. They are based on questionnaires asking soldiers how much pay it would take for them to re-enlist. The validity of any response to such a query is dubious.

The amount of money involved is secondary if there are principled reasons for a voluntary army. But we have obviously reached a point where our resources are strained. We must make a cold-blooded decision between spending our money on armaments or social advancement: on guns or butter. The extra billions are *not* out of line if a volunteer army enhances the prospects of freedom's survival. But they are the cause of deep concern if they merely add to the starvation of a budget already overcommitted to our fighting forces.

The sensible answer is that nobody knows just what it will take to raise an all-volunteer army and nobody is going to know until it is tried. The true cost would be somewhere between that which is hoped for by advocates of the experiment and that which is feared by its opponents. But the issue is moot. At this point, there are no significant political forces urging a real test. All that the administration has put forward are proposals for needed improvements in the present machinery.

This is obvious from a statement to the press prepared by Vice-Admiral William Mack, Acting Assistant Secretary of Defense for Manpower and Reserve Affairs. It was issued on February 18, 1969, *after* President Nixon's inauguration, in a period when pronouncements were no longer in the "campaign oratory" category.

"We are also assuming, as did the President, that the draft authority will be retained," Admiral Mack said. As long as this assumption is valid, neither he nor any other Pentagon manpower expert need change the views they have held for years—views which have produced the system that college youth find so objectionable.

At this point, it might be well to restate the philosophy of the present law. It can be summed up in one sentence: When there is significant fighting, men will be drafted; when things quiet down, they won't—or at least so few will be drafted that no one will notice.

This is not just a philosophy for modern times. It sums up what has been the reality for well over a hundred years—the reality for every war we have fought that has required large numbers of soldiers.

Conscription was introduced to this country during the Civil War—the first conflict that called for the use of large bodies of men over a sustained period of time. It was reintroduced in World War I and World War II. The only really "modern" element is that now we keep the machinery going on a "stand-by" basis in between open hostilities.

Mr. Nixon, in his October, 1968, speech, explained that "we're talking about the same kind of citizen armed force America has had ever since it began, excepting only the period when we have relied on the draft." (To be completely objective, this sentence might have been put into perspective had he pointed out that the reliance upon compulsory service coincided with periods of fighting.)

Actually, of course, Mr. Nixon cannot be "talking about the same kind of citizen armed force America has had ever since it began" with the exception of major war periods. Certainly he does not propose to rest the military establishment of the United States upon state militia units or pre-Civil War Zouave groups—the only true representatives of a "citizen armed force." The "regular" troops of preconscription days consisted largely of hard-bitten professionals—men who regarded themselves as "soldiers" and who were wary of newly entered "civilians."

Our "regular" armies were composed of small cavalry and infantry units who were quickly shunted off to frontier outposts where they could bushwhack Indians and would not annoy civilians. Their major enemies were poorly armed Mexicans or Sioux and Apaches who were still in the Stone Age in a military sense. These soldiers were brave, tough, and able. But to assume that they could be a prototype for a modern military structure staggers the imagination.

A totally "volunteer" army in peacetime is an idea that everyone accepts. In discussing the concept, a better word would be "professional." Nobody is really talking about volunteers. It is clear that there must be professionals who act as caretakers during periods of calm. It is also clear that there must be a body of trained regulars ready to handle the heavy influx of men that are needed to defend the country in time of crisis.

The real argument lies in the concept that the country would be defended solely by professionals in time of war as well. The idea is entitled to examination.

Probably the most persuasive argument against a wholly professional army is that no one can be sure of finding the *right* kind of men at the *right* time through voluntary recruitment. This is the point which is usually effective with Congress and which ultimately brought the Burke Marshall Commission to a unanimous endorsement of Selective Service despite the initial reluctance of some of its members.

Close on the heels of this argument is the fact that a "voluntary" system does not provide adequate machinery for allocating manpower resources in time of war. This was not a major problem in the Korean or Vietnamese conflicts. But it was certainly a problem in World War II and would certainly be a problem again should military needs strain the supply of available men.

Perhaps the strongest argument for Selective Service is that it more efficiently permits the nation to allocate its manpower between those who must fight and those who *must* stay behind to sustain the civilian economy.

Finally, there is the very real problem of where this totally volunteer army will find its base. Historically, "regulars" have been recruited either from families with long military traditions or from sections of the population that are economically depressed and regard military service in the light of economic advancement.

The United States is not a nation with many military families. And when we talk about economically depressed groups in the United States today, we are discussing people who have been so deprived of elementary schooling and the essentials of a decent life that many of them cannot qualify for military service. The Defense Department has experimented successfully with remedial training for the latter group but the experiments have been too limited thus far to permit the conclusion that large, untapped resources of manpower are available. Furthermore, do we want military service to be our only real answer to the poverty problem?

When we say "volunteer army," we are really saying an army composed of the poor and the black. There is no other logical alternative. We are proposing to make military service a career—an objective which in time of peace poses no problems but which in time of war means that we rely on hired hands.

It is passing strange that in these times of concern over the military-industrial complex, so many people are willing to add to the strength of that complex by granting it a mercenary army—one which will be beholden only to its leaders. The advocates of the voluntary army are proposing to give the military establishment something it has never had before—large bodies of trained men who owe their allegiance to the Pentagon only.

And they are doing so without even establishing the certainty that we can raise the voluntary army.

As long as our sights are set on a 2,700,000-man military establishment (which now appears to be the post-Vietnam thinking) the problem is not unmanageable. But this figure is based on the assumption that the professionals will be backed by Selective Service machinery ready to go into action whenever voluntary recruitment fails.

Without that machinery, it must be assumed that the United States will be forced to sustain a much larger military establishment. Only military strategists could give a figure but it is safe to estimate that it would be at least as large as the force presently deployed—3,-500,000 men. And at that figure (or even lower) there is no manpower expert who believes a volunteer force can be raised—although we might come close to it with a major depression.

Against these factors, the arguments of our young people for an all-volunteer army are not likely to be persuasive. This presents a delicate problem. The decisions are going to be made by men and women who are not in danger of being drafted, and this fact alone is enough to widen further the generation gap. There is no way that the older people can abdicate their responsibility for deciding issues. All they can do is to be open and frank about what they're doing and why.

This chapter ends as it began. The young people who believe that the volunteer army is the solution to their difficulties are destined to frustration. It is something that will happen only in time of peace—when they wouldn't be drafted anyway.

It may well be that peace will "break out" in the next few months and that draft calls can be lowered. But this is highly unlikely. Even an end to Vietnam does not necessarily mean an end to large-scale inductions. The terms of those who were drafted two years ago or who enlisted three years ago are coming to an end in a wave. These men must be replaced and there are military planners who believe we are already stretched dangerously thin throughout the world. Nowhere is there an encouraging sign.

Does this mean that Americans are doomed to Selective Service in perpetuity? Of course not. It is even possible that we will see an end to it in our lifetime. But the end will require either technological developments that cannot now be foreseen or a new world order in which nations will find some means of settling disputes other than war.

This, however, is still in the future. The young people of today consider themselves part of the "now" generation and when they are talking about the volunteer army, they are talking "now." And perhaps the greatest contribution to the generation gap has been responding to the "now" with a promise of action in the future.

4

Escape-Hatch Alternatives

As an inveterate and compulsive talker, this writer in the past few years has attended a number of forums entitled "Alternatives to the Draft." Invariably, these meetings break down into either wistful expressions of yearning for a better world or a screaming exchange of invective.

The problem is simply the statement of the subject matter. The audience would participate in the discussion with greater zest if the label were "Alternatives to Being Drafted." And the panelists would probably shed more light if they came prepared to argue "Alternatives to Foreign Policy."

It is highly unlikely, however, that such forums will diminish in popularity or change their direction as long as men are being drafted to fight. The search for "alternatives" has always been rejected in the past by objective analysis, and the conditions which led to the

59

rejection have not changed. But the search for an alternative will continue because the motivation is deeper than a mere desire to avoid military service.

Both the Korean and the Vietnamese wars have presented this nation with painful moral dilemmas. The consciences of millions of Americans—and the number includes this writer—have been troubled by our inability to devise a reasonable solution. The problem is that both wars have called upon a minority of our citizens for great sacrifice while the vast majority continued on their way shaken only by minor annoyances.

The Burke Marshall Commission recognized the impact of this dilemma upon our society when it entitled its report: "In Pursuit of Equity: Who Serves When Not All Serve?" But the best response the Commission could give was a proposal that would make all young men eligible for military service equally *vulnerable* to the draft. This solution has the virtue of equalizing the risk even though it does not equalize the sacrifice. Up to this point, it is the closest approach to equity that anyone has achieved.

The inability to find ideal equity has not (and should not have), however, prevented people from seeking such a goal. And a natural path to follow in such a pursuit is that of trying to impose upon others a sacrifice commensurate with that being made by the fighting men. This has provided the springboard for most of the "alternatives."

No one has yet come up with an alternative that

60

truly fits the description. The basic problem is probably that the only way we can really salve our conscience is to devise hazards equal to those faced by a man in combat—and this is patently absurd. It is inconceivable that we will establish artificial contrivances that will kill some of our young people on a selective basis. Anything short of this, however, is short of the objective of equalizing the sacrifice.

It is difficult to take seriously the assertion that three years in the Peace Corps is equal to one year as a combat infantryman in Vietnam. And no one is able to avoid a snicker of derision when he tries to equate wading under fire in a rice paddy with teaching ghetto children their ABC's. If our slogan is to be "tell it like it is," we have no choice other than to obey the logic of our assumptions.

The search for alternatives usually takes the form of seeking work of "national importance" that can be done by our young people on a sacrifice basis. It is usually assumed that this is something our young people want to do and that they will respond eagerly to this call for constructive achievement that will not be performed on a selfish basis. The case was best stated by Sargent Shriver, who was, at the time, Director of the Office of Economic Opportunity and who had been the head of the Peace Corps. ". . . our younger generation needs this opportunity for service," Mr. Shriver said. "They need to be challenged and to have their best capacities released. They need to be asked to do difficult tasks that our country needs to have done. They need to be called to the frontiers of our society and of the world community. They need to discover themselves."

The Burke Marshall Commission rejected the idea of "alternatives" primarily because it could find no way of equating other forms of service with the sacrifice made by the soldier. It had become quite clear, upon a little reflection, that any work of "national importance" performed as a substitute for conscription would be regarded as draft dodging by those who were most directly affected. Young people are less likely to take refuge in euphemisms than a bureaucrat carried away by his speech writer's enthusiasm.

In meeting this point, of course, the Commission used tactful language. The words of the report are worth quoting. "Equality aside, the Commission is not satisfied that the quality and spirit of volunteer programs could be maintained if they were designated draft alternatives," the report said. "It also believes that any alternative system instituted at this time would be discriminatory in that it would exclude men of lower educational levels, since most opportunities for service now exist only for people who have attended or graduated from college."

The Commission went through an interesting exercise in tracking down the specifics of "work of national importance" that needed to be done. It was not difficult to locate unmet needs. They exist throughout our society. The problem was to find unmet needs that could be met by youthful "volunteers" who would devote only two or three years of their lives to the endeavor.

The manpower shortages in our country are glaring. We live in a land that is desperate for laboratory technicians, policemen, firemen, teachers, and social workers. If numbers alone were the problem, we could easily absorb the total output of teen-agers for the next ten years to provide for the needs of our rapidly expanding society. The only problem is that when the needs are pinned down, they turn out to call for career people—for career technicians who are going to devote a lifetime to the work. And by the time they are ready to perform the tasks, they are past the age of military service.

Even the Peace Corps—considered the epitome of the volunteer concept—is generally manned by people beyond the optimum age for conscription.

What has really happened, of course, is that our society no longer rests upon large areas of constructive labor that can be performed by unskilled hands. During the depression, organizations like the Civilian Conservation Corps were able to use thousands of young people in reclaiming the land and rebuilding the forests. But a technological revolution has taken place in the past forty years. To put young people to work at similar tasks today would be to ask them to perform at lower levels of efficiency than is warranted by modern machinery. It would be "arts and crafts" on a large scale and anyone who has ever tried to occupy the time of teen-agers with "made work" will agree that the endeavor is futile.

The Peace Corps has survived precisely because it has not tried to occupy the time of its members with contrived tasks. It has deliberately restricted its recruiting to young people who are prepared to do a specific job that has been identified and needs to be done. The ranks are limited to a few thousand a year who are already trained to a high degree and who are usually agreeing to donate services for which they could, in the normal course of events, command a much higher price. Their morale is high. It is not hard to imagine the impact upon the psychology of these legitimate volunteers if their ranks were suddenly expanded to bring in tens or even hundreds of thousands of nineteen-year-olds who were *not* qualified for the exacting Peace Corps services and who regarded the organization primarily as a refuge from military service.

It is in the Peace Corps example that we can discern the general principle upon which the "alternative service" concept breaks down. It is not really a lack of human ingenuity that prevents us from devising equalizers of sacrifice. It is rather the effort to equate other forms of human activity with defense of the nation that causes the trouble.

There is no need to go deeply into a discussion of ethics in order to reach the conclusion that war can be justified only as a last resort for preserving basic human values. It is not constructive; it does not enhance human life; it does not solve problems; it does not cure social ills; it does not enrich civilization. It is a grim, nasty, dirty business in which men can engage legitimately for no other reason than survival.

To assume that the business of human butchery can be placed on a level with the constructive tasks of civilization is to mock the sacrifice of the soldier and to degrade the work of the builder. It does not lighten the burdens of the fighting man to know that those at home are wearing a hair shirt and it does not salve the conscience of the civilian to feel that he is teaching slum children to read as an escape from exposure to physical peril.

Sensitive men cannot avoid the thought that work of national importance should be performed because of need—and not because it enables men to escape the fighting.

If the discussions on "alternatives to the draft" were truly motivated by a desire to find a more effective and more equitable military manpower system, it is entirely possible that they would be fruitful. But few, if any, of them are of that character, and it is inevitable that they end in frustration.

The logic of those who seek "constructive alternatives" compels them into strange paths. Inevitably, they must reach the conclusion that our society can compel people to perform a wide variety of services from emptying bedpans in a hospital to constructing sewage systems in India. And the justification is that if men can be compelled to do destructive work, they should also be compelled to do constructive work.

It is unlikely that very many Americans will buy this proposition. This is a nation which has accepted Selective Service only with the greatest reluctance. We have agreed to military compulsion because we thought it was essential to survival. And the national distaste for compulsion is not going to be ameliorated by extending compulsion into other fields.

If there were a burning desire on the part of our young people to engage in social crusades, this factor might lead to the establishment of "alternatives." But it takes considerable imagination to discern this desire among our youth—either on college campuses or elsewhere. It does not take a Gallup Poll to find out that most of them just want to be left alone so they can go about their business—a perfectly legitimate desire.

The current surge of interest in Selective Service alternatives is motivated primarily by the protests of college students. Therefore, it is not possible to discuss the issues without laying a heavy, almost undue, emphasis on their attitudes and on the impact that compulsory military service has on their careers.

The student attitude is unmistakable. This writer has not been on Deep South campuses or visited schools with a strong military tradition such as VMI or Texas A&M. But an extremely clear picture has emerged from innumerable discussions with students and faculty members in the East, the Middle West, and the Far West. The overwhelming mass of students simply does not want to serve and considers any type of avoidance, as long as it is within the law, entirely legitimate.

On the surface, this reaction would appear to reflect deep-seated opposition to the American presence in Vietnam. The student Left, although it is otherwise devoid of Marxist economics and philosophy, has rediscovered the old-fashioned Marxist theory of imperialist war and has applied it to the conflict. Articulate spokesmen of Students for a Democratic Society dominate campus meetings on compulsory military service and speakers must face their sharp questioning, even at conservative schools. Draft-card burnings and draft-board sit-ins are so dramatic that they create the impression that they express college attitudes.

Individual conversations with students outside of formal meeting halls, however, disclose quite a different reaction. The student Left, which in some respects is actually the most traditionalist element of college life, is not speaking for very many young people on this subject. The opposition to compulsory service rests far more upon a feeling that the war is distasteful than a feeling that the war is immoral. The attitude, which is encountered so many times that it is predictable, is simply: what does this have to do with me?

Very few students make the connection, automatic to earlier generations, between fighting behind the American flag and defending freedom. At best, they regard the war in Vietnam as merely another activity of government and see no more reason why they should be compelled to take part in it than that they should be compelled to collect garbage or pave a highway. It is a matter of career choice and they do not regard hunting Vietcong in a jungle under hostile fire as a career with rewards commensurate with the work they have put into their education.

The concept that there is an obligation to fight for the country is alien to student intellectual life, so alien that schemes to avoid the draft are debated quite openly and without the slightest trace of self-consciousness. A disinclination for combat is not regarded as a reflection on a young man's virility and can be discussed without hypocrisy—an attitude disturbing to many older people but which at least is refreshing.

Some of the students assert a willingness to serve the country in what seems to them a positive manner, although the enthusiasm for such service is hardly overwhelming. But their definition of the word positive is limited to social work and teaching. It very definitely does not include army service.

An older generation, which equated manhood with a willingness to plunge into combat, is quite likely to interpret this attitude as indicating deterioration in moral fiber. If it does, it is quite wide of the mark. This writer believes that a more valid appraisal would be that this society has failed to convince its youth that there is any connection between the military establishment and the values of Western civilization. The older generation has either lost its capacity to explain the realities of national life or has adopted mistaken policies which cannot be explained.

The view of Vietnam from the college campus is one of remote horror, as though seen through the wrong end of a telescope. Students are reluctantly willing to concede that there may be pros as well as cons to the war. But under no circumstances can they see a stand on the Mekong River as a defense of their homes in Chicago or a charge through the streets of Hue as an enrichment of their lives. Either act might advance the interests of the United States, in their view, but, if so, the United States should handle it the same way it eradicated cattle tick fever from the Southwest—hire professionals and pay them for the job.

This book is devoted to the problems of a military manpower policy and cannot digress into problems of international policy or education. However, these cannot be ignored in the overall consideration of what we must do. It is not difficult to draw up ideal blueprints which will meet all the technical requirements. But these blueprints must rest upon public acceptance and upon an agreement by our young people that the sacrifice which is asked of them has relevance to their existence as human beings.

For whatever reasons—wrong policies or wrong explanations—this does not describe their current mood. And the attacks on Selective Service are motivated far

69

more by its seeming irrelevancy than by the real inequities which unquestionably have attended its operation.

It is always hard for Americans to admit to themselves that there are problems which really have no solution unless they are considered in a larger context. The moral dilemma posed by the draft is in that category. There is really nothing to be done about it except to make the best out of a bad business—unless we are willing to make some basic changes in our world position.

As long as we are willing to engage in "limited wars," we are going to face the dilemma of thrusting a disproportionate sacrifice upon a minority of our population. This is neither a plea to fight larger wars nor to retreat to isolation. It is merely a statement of a logical conclusion.

War under any circumstances, of course, involves an unequal sharing of the burdens. This was true even in World War II where only a small minority of the 12,000,000 men who were mobilized ever saw actual combat. But this type of war at least puts everyone in a position where he or she can feel a form of participation. Even this is denied to most of our citizens when our country is fighting in Korea or Vietnam. The real problem is not in Selective Service but in our response to the world situation. Conscription is merely a tool which provides men for our armed forces. As long as it is administered equitably, it does not truly pose moral issues. Those are raised in assessing the purposes for which we are raising our armies and the uses to which we are putting them.

There will always, it is to be hoped, persist the yearning dream that men will pour the same energy, determination, and ingenuity into the tasks of peace. This is a noble goal worthy of unrelenting pursuit. But it will not be achieved by opening social work as an escape hatch from grim and dangerous duty. If we are to find an answer to our dilemma, we must look elsewhere. It does not lie in this direction.

5

Random Selection—An Approach to Equity

The thesis of this book is that no "good" answer really exists to the problems of military manpower and that we can only make the best out of a bad situation. It cannot be said with validity that we have done so.

Under any circumstances, Selective Service (or any other system) will be marked by inequities which can be endured only on the grounds of overriding necessity. War is unfair and irrational and neither the unfairness nor the irrationality can be corrected through the machinery that feeds men into it.

There is no difficulty, however, in drawing up an indictment of the present system on the basis of inequities which *can* be corrected. And it can also be charged, with ample justification, that the current law poses a threat to the integrity of our educational system and fails to assure our armed services an adequate supply of the *kind* of men that are needed.

Selective Service, as it now stands, meets just one of the major tests of a military manpower structure. It can provide the *number* of live, healthy bodies requested by the Defense Department at the proper place and at the proper time. If there were no human considerations, the national debate would be unnecessary.

Defects, however, upon which virtually all critics of the system can agree, add up to an impressive list. There is no need to pad it by citing disputed criticisms in order to make a case.

1. The system does not expose all qualified men equally to the risk of induction but provides legal havens for some.

2. The system is erratic in its operation, drafting men in some areas of the country who would be deferred in others.

3. The system keeps our young people in a prolonged state of anxiety, unable to make coherent plans for the future.

4. The system, if it followed the letter of the law, would quickly empty all but our medical and dental graduate schools of able-bodied men and create a serious gap in our intellectual resources.

5. The system, if it followed the letter of the law, would fill the military ranks with overly qualified men at an age when there would be maximum discontent over a crucial interruption to their lifetime career plans.

These defects do not generally flow from inefficiency in administration, although this is a factor in individual instances. It cannot be stressed too heavily that the men who operate the system know their business. Failure to realize this point has undermined the position of far too many critics when they have tested their concepts before Congress. The inequities and the deficiencies are inherent to the machinery itself. They can be corrected only by a fundamental change in the structure and that can come about only through the public acceptance of certain basic realities.

The key to the problem rests in the fact that in the past twenty years we have committed ourselves to two wars which required much less manpower than was available. No one can state with any certainty that it will not happen again—and it must not be forgotten that the second of those wars is still with us.

In his October, 1968, speech, President Nixon quite rightly pointed out that the "problem" of manpower oversupply will become more, rather than less, acute as time passes by. Our population is expanding and we can expect greater numbers of draft-age youths to appear on the scene. For the next decade, the number of nine-teen-year-olds who come of age will be somewhere between 1,800,000 and 2,000,000 annually—and the armed services expect on the average to bid for only about one-third.

A prolonged period of peace would enable the country to rely upon professionals presumably attracted to a military career by the better pay and improved career benefits which Mr. Nixon is seeking. But the acceptability of a military manpower system rests on its reaction to war, not on its operation in peacetime. The professionals are expected only to absorb the first shock of attack and to act as a base upon which a citizen army can be built quickly. There are no plans with respectable backing inside the government to defend the country solely with volunteers.

Furthermore, even given a period when we can rely on professionals, we cannot wait for an emergency to devise and put into operation a draft system. President Nixon has said that Selective Service will be placed on a "stand-by" basis. This appears to mean that it will continue to register and classify men—because these are the time-consuming aspects of compulsory service—in order to be in a position to mobilize them quickly in an emergency.

For some inexplicable reason, the public debate all too often slips away from the issue that is basic to any military manpower policy. The objective of the whole exercise is not to provide careers for some of our citizens but to determine who should do the fighting when fighting is necessary and who should be prepared for fighting in time of peace. And the problem that must be solved is how to provide the most effective method of making that determination consistent with our democratic institutions.

There is universal agreement among all who have made thorough studies that the preferable conscription policy is to draft men at nineteen. The case is so overwhelming that it was accepted even by members of Congress who then proceeded to establish machinery which made the nineteen-year-old draft impossible.

There are a number of reasons for this conclusion. Some of them are negative. A nineteen-year-old youth is least likely to be essential to the support of his family; least likely to be engaged in an essential industry in a capacity where the loss of his services can be disruptive; least likely to have firm career plans where an interruption can be catastrophic. Basically, he is blessed with the resiliency of youth and can snap back much more quickly than his older brothers.

There are also positive reasons that make nineteen years the best age for a draftee. There is a fair chance that he has hit the gap between high school and college (generally considered by educators as the best point for an interruption); he is at the height of his physical prowess; he is more likely to accept military discipline; and the odds are excellent that he can go through a period of service unscarred either physically or psychologically. In many respects, he is the ideal soldier, looking forward to becoming a civilian just as soon as possible.

Of course, there must be certain exceptions. The armed services need a small number of older men—college graduates who have picked up the special skills required to operate a modern military machine. The most important is that of the junior officer—dispensable as an individual but absolutely indispensable as a class.

The armed services count on recruiting 80 per cent of their officers annually from college programs, especially ROTC. There is no assurance that these officers will be available without the pressures of Selective Service. Therefore, the Pentagon is entirely willing to grant undergraduate deferments—not because there is any desire to give undergraduates a break but simply as a method of keeping officer programs alive. If there were no undergraduate deferments, this would mean that college students had either been drafted and served their time or that they had escaped the draft and could not be made vulnerable a second time.

This introduces the concept of the "constructive" nineteen-year-old. This word, which is used frequently in discussions of manpower problems, means simply that the law regards any student who has finished his college education as being of draft age. His name goes into the manpower pool along with the nineteen-year-olds and he has the same vulnerability to service. No one has really done him any favor. He was merely reserved for future military need.

The undergraduate college deferment troubles many people from the standpoint of equity. Obviously, it means that young people who are not going to college have no choice other than to submit to the Selective Service process, whereas others may defer themselves out of a time of peril. There is no answer to this criticism other than to point out that they are deferring themselves *into* another period which might be a time of even greater peril. It is doubtful whether those who took advantage of the education deferment in 1963 or 1964, when things were relatively quiet, feel so happy about their choice today.

This, of course, is a digression. It leads away from the central fact that the nineteen-year-old draft has been endorsed by the Burke Marshall Commission; the House Advisory Commission; the Senate Armed Services Committee; the House Armed Services Committee; and the former President of the United States. There is scarcely a dissenting voice in official circles.

The voices of dissent, however, become quite vociferous when it comes to passing the legislation that will enable the nineteen-year-old draft to operate. There is strong reluctance emotionally to drafting teen-agers for combat. Here is an area in which many men are incapable of following through the logical implications of their own thinking.

The present system of drafting the oldest first was workable, though inequitable, in the past because it was coupled with a policy of generous deferments. This enabled draft boards to by-pass the older and less desirable men and reach down into younger age groups. A clever and reasonably determined man could avoid conscription permanently merely by going to school until he was twenty-six years old, picking up a wife and a couple of children along the way. No single act would excuse him from military service. But it was not at all difficult to pyramid deferments, one on top of another, until he had reached an age when the military was no longer interested.

Draft calls were so low that nobody really cared in the late 1950's and early 1960's. The pyramiding of deferments was regarded as entirely legitimate—and some people even defended the system on the grounds that it made a positive contribution to higher education. Many young men stayed in college for a Ph.D. because it was more desirable than an army serial number.

The soaring casualty rates in Vietnam made this state of affairs intolerable to most Americans. It was not possible to justify a system in which some young men could buy their way out of a hazard that should be shared by all with the price of a college tuition fee. The Burke Marshall Commission recommended strongly that virtually all deferments be abolished (there was a dispute over undergraduate college deferments) and that under any circumstances pyramiding of them be stopped. Virtually everyone—executive and legislative— agreed, *in principle*.

In practice, however, the law that was enacted on this assumption included elements that undermined the whole concept. Congress insisted on retention of the practice whereby the oldest eligible men were to be called first, although some discretion was left to the President to issue calls by age groups. This posed a baffling quandary to the Selective Service system. There were some 700,000 male students in the nation's graduate schools. To abolish their deferments and draft them immediately would flood the ranks with M.A. and Ph.D. candidates—a prospect horrifying to drill sergeants and college professors alike.

The operations of the law have yet to produce a full-scale migration of graduate students from campus dormitories to military barracks—largely because draft boards have been slow to reshuffle their files and have insisted on using their discretionary power to maintain occupational deferments. But obviously the law is not being enforced in the spirit in which it was conceived, and it hangs as a threat over both the educational system and the military structure. Literal adherence to the language of the act would empty graduate classrooms of all but IV-F's and women and fill the ranks with disgruntled soldiers.

The nineteen-year-old draft would be a solution to this problem, and the solution would not be complicated by the use of the undergraduate deferment. In practice, it would mean that graduate students would have their military obligations behind them and could plan their lives on the basis of taking up a civilian career as soon as they had completed their scholastic work. Only medical and dental students would be contemplating a post-degree military tour, and this is not a factor which differs from that which they face now.

There would be problems of transition from the current system to a nineteen-year-old draft. None of these is insurmountable.

But the operation of the nineteen-year-old draft

presents a problem. It is how the Selective Service can differentiate among men of the same age group who fall within the range of military acceptability. The armed services can reject only about one-third of those examined for physical, educational, psychological, or moral reasons. With about 1,800,000 becoming nineteen every year, this leaves twice the number that can be used.

The dilemma is a painful one. Somehow, young men to the number of 1,200,000 must be lined up every year and half of them told to grab rifles as an introductory step to ambushing Vietcong detachments. The other half can only be told to go home—"we will call you if we need you."

These young men are all roughly equal. They vary within a range because human beings vary. But they have enough health, intelligence, and physical agility to serve their country. There is no way in which they can be separated objectively into cannon fodder and noncannon fodder. And human beings, confronted with such problems, traditionally fall back on spinning a bottle or a wheel.

Unfortunately, it is not at all easy to convince the average American that this is the only way out. The reactions of Congress and the reactions of the polls combine to register deep-seated objections to the "lottery." People do not like to think that someone is going to shoot cosmic craps to settle the fate of their sons even though this principle was accepted without many qualms in World War II. And it is idle to deplore this attitude as illogical or ill-founded.

The random selection system, however, when emotional language is eliminated, is merely an impersonal method of making choices—one that eliminates the possibility of favoritism in designating men to perform an unpleasant or hazardous job. The only conceivable alternative, in this instance, is to authorize someone to make the choice on the basis of individual preference, a power which should be granted to no human being.

The nineteen-year-old draft will not work without a random selection system. This might be a lottery or any one of a number of mathematical devices. The only requirement is that it be a mechanism which eliminates the possibility of favoritism. This point is so important that it is worth a detailed explanation of how it works.

The random selection system does NOT determine who is eligible but *who among those equally eligible shall serve when all are not needed*. Therefore, the first step is an objective determination of which nineteen-year-olds are eligible for the draft "pool" and which, for compelling reasons, should be eliminated— either permanently or temporarily. The latter would include those who had medical, psychological, or educational deficiencies; "hardship" cases (which will exist even with nineteen-year-olds); conscientious objectors; and whatever other deferments and exemptions can be impartially granted.

Those remaining in the pool of eligibles and those

placed in the pool from past deferments which had expired would be considered alike in terms of vulnerability to service. If the number is equal to the military need, there is no problem. They all go. But if the number is greater than the military need, some method must be found to decide the order in which they are to be called.

The simplest way of solving the problem is to place in a drum the number that each individual was assigned when he registered with Selective Service and then draw all the numbers one at a time. The order in which they would be drawn would determine the order in which eligibles would be called to service. Those who were drawn early, of course, would be virtually certain to be called; those whose numbers appeared towards the end of the draw would be virtually certain to be excused.

The order in which the numbers were drawn would remain valid for a year. Then they would be retired and a new set of nineteen-year-olds (again, plus those whose deferments had expired) would be placed in the pool. Those who had not been inducted could then count on immunity except in case of a truly major conflict in which no able-bodied citizen would escape.

Any mathematician can cite innumerable variations on the system outlined above. There is no point in going into them here. Whether they be the "conveyor belt" procedure outlined by the House Armed Services Committee in 1967 or the monthly number publication procedure proposed by Senator Kennedy of Massachusetts, they come to the same thing. They set forth the only device yet known to differentiate between men who otherwise have been determined to be equally eligible for an unwanted duty.

From the standpoint of the prospective draftee, the advantage of the system is significant. It does not equalize the sacrifice but it does equalize the risk of sacrifice. It does not make an unpleasant duty any less unpleasant but it does eliminate the element of uncertainty. The young man who has been subjected to the process *knows* whether he must plan his life around a two-year tour of duty in the armed services or whether he can eliminate this prospect from his considerations altogether.

The institution of a random selection system would also solve another basic problem. It is the disposition of the large number of graduate students who piled up during the many years that they were granted deferments during the Vietnamese war.

At the time of this writing, there are about 700,000 of them hanging over the military manpower pool. It is inconceivable that graduate deferments—which were supposedly eliminated in most cases after the 1967 act —can be continued. The undergraduate deferment can be justified on the basis of military necessity. The graduate deferment becomes all too easily a method of dodging the draft—one that cannot be justified while other young men are fighting and dying.

From the standpoint of equity, these men cannot be relieved of some military obligation. To do so would confirm a suspicion that the draft is a device to ensure a "rich man's war and a poor man's fight." There is only one conceivable middle ground between taking all of them and excusing them completely. That is to subject this group plus the nineteen-year-olds to random selection in one operation and thereafter to proceed on the basis of the nineteen-year-old draft (keeping in mind the concept of the "constructive" nineteen-year-old as explained earlier). This would mean that a fair proportion would be conscripted and the rest could go about their business. The problem would not arise again because the graduate students of the future would be past the period of maximum vulnerability. They would have discharged their military obligations to the country.

All the problems of Selective Service, of course, would not be solved by the random selection method. Nevertheless, it is basic to the solutions that now appear to be available. For this reason, it has been granted a separate chapter in this book. The other problems will be discussed in the chapter to follow.

Whether the objections to random selection can be overcome cannot now be foreseen. The system has been labeled "the lottery" and the label cannot be removed. As such, it runs counter to deep-seated emotions in our society.

Without some such device, however, it is difficult to see how the basic problem can be solved. When our military manpower resources outstrip our military manpower needs, there appears to be no alternative method of selection. It is either blind chance or favoritism, and while the first is distasteful the second is an option with which no democratic society can long live.

6
Your Friendly, Neighborly Board

The administrative defects of the Selective Service system flow, almost without exception, from unyielding efforts to sustain a myth. It is that the decisions on who will do the fighting are made by committees of "friends and neighbors" of the nation's youth.

The myth never had much substance behind it at any time during the twenty-nine-year history of the present system. This writer, a World War II draftee, was just barely aware of the physical location of his draft board and never bothered to learn the names of its members. The whole transaction, except for registration and a physical examination, was handled by mail. This has been the experience of the overwhelming majority of soldiers who entered the ranks through conscription.

The double-barreled premise of the "friends and neighbors" concept is laudable and in a different kind of society would afford a healthy base for a compulsory system of military service. The assumption is that the community conscience represents the strongest safeguard against favoritism and bias and that neighborhood boards would be the best custodians of that conscience. It is also assumed that men entering the armed forces through a community decision are likely to regard themselves as selected defenders of their homes rather than as mercenaries forced unwillingly into combat.

The problems created by the local boards arise not because the premise is illogical but because it bears virtually no relationship to the realities of modern life. In rural and small-town America, the boards may operate in the idyllic pattern foreseen by the framers of the law. But rural America, in the sense of regions populated by family farms, and small-town America, in the sense of communities serving farm families, is almost a thing of the past. The overwhelming majority of Americans are urbanites or suburbanites—living in a society of anonymity where even the man next door may not be a "neighbor" but only another occupant of a "housing unit."

Revealing comments on the friendly and neighborly character of the local draft boards were made by nine college students who toured campuses under the auspices of the Burke Marshall Commission. One of them described the identity of board members as "one of the best guarded secrets in America." Another said: "The idea that the draft boards are a group of your neighbors sitting in judgment or consideration of your fate is not a workable real plan right now. No one seems to know who the members of his draft board are."

The student attitude is a reaction to impersonality— a characteristic diametrically opposed to the fundamental concepts upon which the boards were established.

The students are not alone in this feeling that the machine is anonymous. During the deliberations of the Commission, the Office of Economic Opportunity brought to Washington a large group of citizens representing impoverished areas and made them available for questioning by this writer (then acting as a Commission member). Only a few Mexican-Americans and Indians from rural areas of the Southwest could actually name any of their draft board members.

It should be added, however, that in contrast to the college students there was surprisingly little bitterness expressed against the Selective Service system or the boards by this group. The cynical remarks of the poverty leaders were directed instead at National Guard and Regular Reserve recruitment programs, for reasons that will be discussed in the next chapter.

The concept of the local board actually grew out of the Civil War, which provided this nation with its first experiment in formal conscription. This was not a very successful experiment. The methods were poorly conceived and even permitted those with enough money to hire a substitute if they drew an "unlucky" number. The draft riots in New York City, among the most savage internal eruptions in our history, were unmistakable evidence that compulsory military systems could work only if citizens had confidence in their administration. Thoughtful men, reflecting on the painful experience, recommended that future conscription be placed in the hands of committees of "civilian neighbors." This idea, developed in an America still largely rural, has dominated the laws on the subject to this highly urbanized day.

In practice, the modern Selective Service system rests upon some 4,000 draft boards scattered around the country and possessed of an incredible degree of autonomy. They vary widely in the size of their geographical jurisdiction, the number of registrants under their control, and their administration of classification procedures. The Burke Marshall Commission found a board in Hinsdale County, Colorado, with 28 registrants whereas the board in North Hollywood, California, had 54,323.

The Commission undertook the only comprehensive and systematic study of the boards that has been attempted in recent years. The results, even though obscured by the deadening monotony required in government reports, made fascinating reading. The picture painted was that of groups composed exclusively of men, nearly all white, elderly, and well-entrenched in their positions.

At the time the survey was made, the average age of

the board members was fifty-eight. One-fifth of the board members were over seventy, including 400 who were over eighty and 12 over ninety. A more important factor than age, however, was that almost half of the board members had served for more than ten years and 8 per cent of them had served more than twenty years.

In terms of racial composition, only 1.3 per cent were black; 0.8 per cent Puerto Rican; 0.7 Spanish-American. Orientals and American Indians were minuscule—0.2 per cent for the former and 0.1 per cent for the latter. Generally speaking, board members were in white-collar occupations or in the professions, with only a small minority of craftsmen, semiskilled workers, and laborers.

It would take an incredible leap of the imagination to picture these men as representative of American society generally—let alone as representative of the young people who are called upon to do the fighting. Certainly, the elderly, the educated, the white, and the well-born are overrepresented; whereas the young, the halftaught, the nonwhite, and the lowly have reason to feel that they cannot experience much empathy with these "friends and neighbors." The situation has improved considerably since the survey was made but it is still far short of equitable representation.

It should be stressed that there is very little reason to doubt the integrity of the boards. The system, for one which has dealt with such a highly emotional issue for nearly three decades, has been remarkably free of charges of scandal. The cynicism that young people express in their discussion of Selective Service usually centers around the conviction that board members are biased and incapable of understanding modern problems—not that they are dishonest. College students especially tend to regard them as the epitome of "the establishment"—that presumed conspiracy of adults to frustrate youthful efforts for happiness and a meaningful life.

The idea that there is a conscious desire on the part of board members to frustrate young America is sheer nonsense. But the board members *do* have a very human tendency (shared by far younger people) to interpret problems in terms that match their own experience and environment. And this means that people who can communicate with them in those terms are more likely to receive a favorable hearing. Boards in high-income areas are far more likely to grant student deferments than those in low-income areas. And a board in a region dominated by Mennonites is likely to pass out conscientious objector classifications which, in another place, would certainly be rejected at the local level though sustained on appeal.

Of course, about 90 per cent of the board work is routine. And the appeals system that has been established by Selective Service works quite well—provided the selectee knows it exists. The more important factor is that the boards represent a powerful, conservative force highly resistant to change. They form a nationwide network of influential, even though somewhat anonymous, citizens ready to throw their very considerable influence behind General Hershey at any time. And they, like General Hershey, are quite likely to interpret proposals for change as an intentional slur on their integrity.

The principal problem created by the local board system is lack of uniformity in classification and deferment policies. There is absolutely no rule upon which a youth can rely confidently as to whether he can be deferred for certain activities. Attitudes vary from board to board and are only partially checked by national directives. The geographical accident of residence at time of registration may well determine whether a young man will enter the armed forces or pursue a civilian career in peace.

One draft board may defer auto mechanics; another declare them nonessential. A school teacher may be "safe" in one area and hauled into service in the next county. There are boards which have granted hundreds of conscientious objector deferments, and others which have refused all such applications even though many of the rejected applicants later received the classification on appeal. And a student who can maintain his II-S deferment with twelve semester hours in one state may have to carry fifteen in another as the only alternative to carrying a rifle.

The extent to which this condition could be cured by directives from Selective Service headquarters is open to dispute. But it is doubtful whether full uniformity could be reached under any circumstances. The members of the boards are neither government officials nor government employees. They are people who are donating their time to a rather thankless job and are beholden only to their own consciences in interpreting the law *and* the directives which come to them from national and state headquarters. It would be surprising if they did not vary even in their interpretations of rulings sent out to secure uniformity.

Furthermore, the government has not been very generous in supplying the board with the kind of help that would assure maximum efficiency. The heart—as well as the body—of the paid board staff is a clerk who, until recently, was paid at levels well below those set for comparable federal workers. For all practical purposes, this clerk performs the initial classification of the registrant and has little time to take away from filing duties.

All of these circumstances combine to give the individual board members a feeling of great independence from the federal government. In addition, they have been indoctrinated for many years with the concept that they are representatives of a community—and should make their decisions in the light of their interpretation of "local" needs.

To the prospective draftee, the system is little short of bewildering. He is presented with papers to sign and questionnaires to answer. He is aware that the course of his whole life will depend upon his responses. But until recently he had no reliable guidance in seeking words which would lead him in the direction that he wants to go or is entitled to go. At the urging of the Burke Marshall Commission, Selective Service now supplies registrants with information explaining the appeals system in relatively clear English.

Even so, the process is still painful. Under the rhetoric of the Selective Service Act, at least one of the board members should be a "friend and neighbor" with whom he can speak directly. But there is very little effort to sustain this fiction at the time of registration. If the young man is a resident of a big city, he will probably find that the board offices are not even in his quarter of the town, let alone in his neighborhood. The members have taken the sensible step of moving into a central office along with the other metropolitan draft boards where the clerks can share some of the work and the burdens be lightened.

The prospective draftee who feels that he has not had a fair break has quite a few opportunities for appeal. He can appear before the board that made the decision; he can appeal to a state appeals board; he can appeal to the President. The system, however, is subject to valid criticism in that many of the legal safeguards fall far short of those available in a court of law and officials have only recently provided young people with the kind of information they really need to understand their rights. The more valid criticism is that the system is far too complex and creates inequities merely by its structure.

It is not a very difficult task to devise a uniform system, providing that it is based upon the nineteen-year-old draft and an almost complete absence of deferments. The Burke Marshall Commission recommendation in this area is typical of a number of proposals, although it is not the only way of getting at the problem.

The Commission proposed to consolidate the operations of the Selective Service system into eight regional offices which would administer 300 to 500 area offices. These would be distributed according to population rather than geography (although it was recommended that there be at least one in each state).

This type of organization would permit adequate staffing of the area offices where the eighteen-year-olds would register and be classified. It would be possible with this kind of consolidation to ensure the presence of full-time counsellors, including appeals agents specifically charged with guiding those who wished to object.

The Burke Marshall Commission proposed that the local boards remain in existence but only to serve as a first step in the appeals process. The next step would be a regional appeals board and finally the national board itself.

It is obvious that this kind of organization could be administered with a high degree of efficiency. Computer equipment, so dear to the hearts of modern administrators, could be employed effectively, and professionals could be concentrated effectively in a manner not possible when the whole system rests upon more than 4,000 individual boards. But more important than efficiency is the fact that a consolidated system could be operated more equitably.

The ticklish problems of classification would be handled by experts. But the human factor would be maintained by the use of the draft board as an appeal board. It might not be a committee of friends and neighbors but it does have the virtue of standing outside the government. The work load could be distributed more evenly and there would be fewer cases of small boards forced to take men in categories deferred in other areas.

It is quite obvious that if Selective Service is to continue, there must be some form of consolidation. The current distribution of 4,000 boards on a geographical basis simply does not fit the shape of our country. The problem of supplying manpower for our armed forces is a question of population and not of geography. To administer boards varying from 28 to 54,000 registrants (admittedly an extreme, but 985 boards have fewer than 5,000 and 103 have more than 25,000) is to administer a monstrosity.

Again, the same caution must be issued as in the previous chapter. Administrative reform will still leave considerable room for unfairness—simply because war is inequitable and cannot be made otherwise. But the system can be modernized and made more equitable and thereby recapture much of the respect it has lost.

There is no technique of administration, human engineering, or public relations which can make military service palatable in a non-Spartan society. But if the system is workable and as fair as human ingenuity can make it, respect can be achieved and with respect comes acceptability.

The local board structure in a highly mobile, industrial environment is in effect a challenge to young people to exercise their wits against the "Establishment." Many of them will succeed either through native cunning or geographical "luck." Others will fail, either through lack of alertness and personal resources or through sheer happenstance. Neither situation is healthy in a country which needs today, more than any other quality that could be bestowed upon it, confidence in itself and confidence in its leaders.

7
The Role of the Minorities

One of the most perplexing issues in the debate on conscription is whether the Selective Service system discriminates against minority groups. The general assumption is that it does. But the available facts are inconclusive. By careful selection of statistics, a speaker can "prove" any viewpoint that coincides with his prejudices.

The Burke Marshall Commission made a careful analysis of the position of Negroes in the draft board set-up. The members of the Commission emerged from the study baffled and extremely cautious about drawing any conclusions. The one thing that was clear was that the figures could speak either way, and the report offered the guess that the same would be true for other minority groups.

There is no doubt that black participation in the draft structure reflects a position of inequity. But that is not the issue. The real question is whether the inequities flow from overall discrimination by our society or whether they can be pinned down specifically to the Selective Service system.

From the standpoint of membership on the local boards that do the drafting, Negroes are obviously un-derrepresented—at the time of the Burke Marshall study only 1.3 per cent of the board members were black compared with 10 or 11 per cent blacks in the total population. On the other hand, these boards cannot have been too discriminatory because Negroes serve in the armed forces in proportion to their percentage among the general public. In the army, however, their percentage is somewhat higher.

The figures most often cited to prove discrimination are the casualty rates in Vietnam. The study used by the Burke Marshall Commission showed that in the first eleven months of 1966, more than 22 per cent of the soldiers killed in that war were Negro. On the other hand, Negroes apparently had a greater tendency than whites to volunteer for the elite combat units which were most likely to be exposed to extreme danger. There were airborne divisions (which rely exclusively on volunteers) that were 24 per cent black—more than twice their proportion in the general population.

All these facts can be interpreted in accordance with the preconceptions of the interpreter. It can be said, perhaps with validity, that Negroes prefer paratroop organizations because once inside they find a complete absence of discrimination and a tendency to color-blindness on the part of their superiors. It can also be said, perhaps with equal validity, that Negroes gravitate to the elite fighting outfits because they have been deprived of the education that would make advancement possible in more technically oriented branches of the armed services. The truth may well be a combination of both factors plus the enhanced opportunities afforded by a green beret to express extreme virility—an inducement that must be compelling to men who for 300 years have been forced to conceal even routine masculine impulses.

There is one figure which suggests that discrimination may operate to keep Negroes *out* of military service rather than sweep them in. The black rejection rate is double that of the white. This, of course, is why the percentage of *qualified* Negroes drafted is higher than that of the whites. The larger percentage of disqualifications makes the pool of eligibles smaller. (The rejections are due mostly to failures on the written tests. Many Negroes complain bitterly that the questions are so devised that they are comprehensible only to those emerging from a white culture.)

An important figure is the Negro re-enlistment rate —almost double that of the white. One conclusion can be stated with confidence. It is that black youths are more likely than whites to find a congenial home in the services. This writer leaves it to his readers to determine whether this is cause for praising our Defense Department or deprecating our society.

Perhaps the most important of all the statistical trends is found in the death rate of army Negroes from hostile action in Vietnam. From 1961 to 1966, when most of the soldiers in that area were volunteers, 20 per cent of combat fatalities were black. In 1967, when the composition of our Vietnamese forces was much more heavily draftee, the rate had fallen to 13.5 per cent and in the first nine months of 1968 to 13.3 per cent. It is impossible to escape the conclusion that Selective Service, even when operating under less than ideal circumstances, tends to bring a greater cross section of the population into the fighting forces.

Perhaps the most balanced appraisal would be that the Selective Service system is not discriminatory in and of itself. But it is operating in a social environment shaped by 300 years of legal discrimination in most areas and by *de facto* discrimination in all. We are emerging from that era and have taken long and important steps to abolish inequality in the legal treatment of our citizens. But the institutions inherited from 300 years of enforced inequality are more stubborn and do not yield so easily to executive order or legislative enactment.

Nowhere is this principle better illustrated than in the recruitment of National Guard and Organized Reserve units. The percentage of nonwhites who have succeeded in penetrating the ranks of either group as a method of entering military service is so low that blacks generally regard them as "Jim Crow" outfits. The Burke Marshall Commission estimated that less than 3 per cent of Negro veterans had begun their military careers in the reserves and only in the District of Columbia and New Jersey National Guards were blacks found in significant numbers. Since the Reserves and the Guard units are among the most publicized "escape hatches" from conscription, this causes considerable bitterness.

However, an inquiry into this apparent discrimination discloses some perplexing problems.

A satisfactory reserve policy has been the elusive target of military manpower planners for many years. Up to this writing, no one can claim that the target has been hit. The basic problem arises out of the reservists' character as semisoldier, semicivilian and is complicated in the case of the Guard by the constitutional relationship between federal and state governments.

A reservist is a man who is assuming a long period of military obligation as a part-time soldier in preference to a shorter period of intensive service. He is gambling that his unit will not be ordered to active duty during his tour, and the reluctance of the defense establishment to mobilize Reserve units has made this gamble generally a good one during the Vietnamese war.

To the regular military man, these units are a necessary headache. Their training is sporadic (and sometimes nonexistent); their readiness for combat uncertain; and, since they are composed of weekend soldiers pursuing civilian careers, their morale on active duty generally low. Furthermore, they are not under military discipline to the extent that their residences are subject to control. Civilians have a habit of moving from one place to another in accordance with economic need. As a result, it is hard to keep a unit together as a team.

But to the young man whose neck is being caressed by the hot breath of the draft, the Organized Reserves can appear as an oasis in the desert. The burden that Reserve service imposes, except in full-time active-duty periods, is not very onerous. It consists of a few months of intensive training followed by weekend drills and sporadic tours which rarely last more than a couple of weeks. Obviously, as contrasted to active service in Vietnam, this is a "good deal," and Reserve unit waiting lists have been jammed for the past few years.

The National Guard structure presents similar problems but with an added complication. The units are under the jurisdiction of state governors, with the proviso that they can be "borrowed" by the President in an emergency. Recruitment policies are under state control and can be influenced by the federal government only through negotiation, possibly helped by the judicious use of certain types of federal aid.

It is almost inconceivable that Congress would ever authorize the permanent federalization of the Guard. If it did, this would probably be followed by the creation of state militia units, which is what happened during

World War II. Whatever may be the disadvantages of the federal-state relationship, it is going to be maintained, and no one can deny the states some kind of a military force to preserve internal order.

The result, however, is another "good deal" for the young man looking for an alternative to regular army service. Therefore, the waiting list of applicants for National Guard units has been fully as long as it has been in the Reserves. Also, as in the Reserves, Negro applicants have a tendency to lose out to whites.

The Defense Department, which has proved its good faith by desegregating regular forces, has tried to remedy this discriminatory situation but with only partial success. The efforts have come too late—after the waiting lists were top-heavy with whites who signed up in a period when blacks believed there was no point in even trying. The pattern of discrimination had been in effect for so long that no one could believe in its reversal.

There is another problem for Negroes who want to enlist in Guard or Reserve units. Many of the most desirable openings tend to be for technicians. This is a serious obstacle for many blacks, who have been deprived of the required education. Opening positions on a basis of equal competition means very little to people who have had withheld from them an equal opportunity to prepare for the competition.

One of the more imaginative efforts to meet this problem in the regular services has been Project

100,000, launched by the Defense Department in 1966. This involves a deliberate lowering of acceptance standards to permit the recruitment of men who had been previously rejected for physical or educational reasons *but who could render adequate service after remedial training*. Most of the emphasis has been on correcting educational defects simply because there are too many legal problems involved in correcting physical defects. Frequently the latter requires surgery which can be performed only with the consent of the patient.

In the opinion of the writer, this program has merit and should be continued and expanded. It is an excellent method of using existing facilities to make a dent in a pressing social problem—the educational and physical deprivation of a significant part of our population, both black and white. It adds to the quality of our human resources, not just in terms of war but in the more important terms of peace.

However, Project 100,000 will not be discussed at length here because it does not contribute to a solution of our current Selective Service problem. If anything, it sharpens the dilemma by adding to a pool of manpower that is already too big. This program can "solve" the military manpower quandary only on the assumption that we are preparing the unfortunate and the lowly to do the "dirty work" that the fortunate and the well-born disdain.

The discussion of discrimination, however, would not be complete without noting one ray of light shed

108

by Project 100,000. It is a sharp reminder that the problem of the Negro in regard to the armed services today flows from his poverty more than from his color. This was not the case in the past and, of course, it was the legal treatment he received in the past that led to his present plight. But he is not entirely alone in his present situation—just more visible.

During the first year of Project 100,000 more than 60 per cent of the men accepted into the program were white and less than 37 per cent were black. As whites, these men may have been in a better position than Negroes to secure a "safe" National Guard berth, but as far as the regular army is concerned, they were under the same disability.

The real problem of discrimination, of course, remains unanswered. This is due to the peculiar gyrations of a society whose racial policies are in a state of transition. We have made a national decision to put an end to inequality before the law. But that is quite a different thing, we have discovered, from putting an end to inequality of treatment by institutions.

Traditionally, the army has served as one of the avenues through which some minorities escaped discrimination in this country. Those, however, were different times. Families struggling to keep above the poverty line did not have thrust upon them from every angle the lures of an affluent society with its capacity to create dissatisfaction among the poor. A soldier's life, in an army which did little fighting other than to beat back poorly armed Mexican revolutionaries who crossed the border from time to time, compared favorably with the alternatives *known* to most Americans. Higher education was so exclusively the province of the wealthy and wellborn that it rarely occurred to those at the lower end of the ladder that they should envy those who had access to college campuses.

Furthermore, the Irish boys had a martial tradition. There was always a grandfather who had taken the "Queen's shilling" or an uncle who had wandered through South America as a mercenary. It was a natural development for them but was a path not every minority group wanted to follow.

The modern context is totally different. Military life, at least for the foreseeable future, involves extreme hazard, and it is all too painfully obvious that it does not compare favorably with other career choices available to people who have been "accepted" by our society but who are of modest means. Even steel mills or lumber camps, both now studded with labor-saving devices, are far preferable.

Against this background, the statistics are meaningless as evidence to prove or disprove discrimination. Champions of the thesis that we have made progress will insist that our willingness to accept Negroes in combat units (something we did *not* do in World War II) is a tremendous step forward. Black separatists will counter that it is merely the beginning of another form of Jim Crow—this time accompanied by a long-range commitment to genocide.

The real answer probably lies in judgments that go far beyond the narrow question of military manpower. If we are truly opening the privileges of our society as well as its obligations (and defending our country is an obligation), then Selective Service is nondiscriminatory. But if the only "privilege" we are according is really an obligation, then we will have a heavy burden added to the white conscience.

It seems obvious to this writer that a sincere effort is being made to atone for past wrongs. It is a confused, groping effort that has met only limited success because it is an unprecedented experiment in reversing social relationships for which we have to draw up the blueprints as we go along. Nor is it surprising that the beneficiaries of this change of heart are not particularly grateful. Justice that is granted to complainants after a delay of 300 years is hardly an achievement that makes men sing with joy.

Nevertheless, we cannot make progress unless all men stand equal before the law—sharing both its benefits and its restrictions. And now that we have decided to do away with legal discrimination, the only honorable course is to proceed to treat men equally, in confidence that the institutional barriers will also fall.

8

The Morality of Conscription

The ultimate objective of any military manpower system is to organize our society effectively to commit violence. The exercise, of course, will be performed only under circumstances which lead us to feel that we have ample justification. Even assuming, however, that human wisdom is sufficient to make such a determination correctly in every instance, moral questions remain to be answered. They must never be resolved on the grounds of efficiency.

Aside from the total pacifists, the moral issues are raised most insistently by the campus advocates of the volunteer army. As a practical matter, the voluntarism issue is probably moot. There is very little likelihood that this nation, in the foreseeable future, will give young men an unrestricted choice of becoming or not becoming combat soldiers in time of war. About the best they can realistically expect is a choice of becoming or not becoming professional soldiers in time of peace.

It is no more responsive, however, to dismiss the moral questions on the ground that military voluntarism is moot than on the ground that it is impractical.

Where motives are ascertainable, they probably provide the best basis for a discussion of moral issues. Fortunately, when the voluntary army is the point of the debate, the motives are not obscured in the slightest. The impetus for the movement arises solely out of individual desire to avoid fighting in Vietnam.

There is very little hypocrisy surrounding this motivation. An hour spent on any college campus will bring the subject into sharp focus. No one pretends, even for a moment, that there is any other reason for the heightened interest of students in military manpower policy than the danger of conscription at a time when an unpopular war is being fought.

This can be said without impugning the courage or the integrity of the modern college student. There is no reason to believe that he is any different from his predecessors, except in highly superficial aspects. His attitude towards Selective Service arises from the failure of anyone to convince him that the war is a cause for which he should sacrifice. It is not, on the whole, that he is opposed to it. The war just seems remote from his life or from any values that he considers important.

Those who are genuinely opposed to the war do not

engage in confusing arguments about the virtues of a "voluntary" army or the iniquities of compulsory military service. They merely register a flat dissent to the whole business of fighting—which may be disconcerting to their elders but which can be met head on.

Very little was heard about the "draft" when Selective Service was not conscripting college students or anybody that college students were likely to know. The whole question was merely boring when monthly draft calls were down to 1,500 or zero. It was not until they faced the very real danger of death, disability, or at the very least interruption to their careers that college students began to clamor for "volunteers" and decided that compulsory military service was immoral.

If the movement for a volunteer army had been launched from a genuine desire to devise a more effective or a more equitable military manpower policy for the United States, it would be far more impressive. But the message is quite clear. It arises *solely* from the belief of many of our college students that military service is *distasteful* and should be left to those who have nothing better to do.

In this context—and it is impossible to find any other —the moral issue takes on another coloration. The more fortunate members of our society are proposing that the burden of defending our country be carried by the less fortunate. And, in the course of doing so, they are contributing to the polarization of our nation between the rich and the poor.

The argument that a volunteer army will transform itself into a band of mercenaries who can be used to abolish our freedoms is somewhat tendentious. But it is quite possible that the same impulse that seeks to shrug off the responsibilities of defending our society, by relegating the task to a professional army, can accomplish that end. And it is idle to deny that a change at this point would alter drastically the relationships between the civilian and the military sectors of our nation.

Our current military system, for all its faults, is based upon relationships that seem to this writer to be healthy and moral. Our professional soldiers are custodians of the defensive potential of the country—maintaining continuity, studying the arts of war, and remaining ready to absorb the first shock of an attack. But it is clearly understood that a major emergency will activate the machinery that brings into being a citizen army composed of men who are fighting because the nation must fight but who are civilians at heart and planning to return to a civilian life as soon as they can. A citizen army in the modern age can be achieved only through organization which decides who will wear the uniform and who will keep the economy going. This is a choice that must be made by the community. Individuals cannot make it for themselves.

One wonders what would be the psychological impact on our soldiers of a switch to a "volunteer" army with the idea that defending our nation is "dirty work"

116

not to be done by those who have better options. It is impossible to engage in such speculation with any degree of comfort. A democratic society cannot rest upon such a foundation.

The moral argument advanced by supporters of the voluntary army is that it is wrong to compel a man to risk his life against his will. This is a thesis which has a great deal of appeal to any individual. But the problem of compulsion has been settled long since in our society. We compel people to do many things that they do not want to do—even acts which trouble their consciences deeply. A citizen must pay taxes—even though the money is used for purposes to which he objects strongly. A citizen must send his children to school— even though he may have intense religious convictions to the contrary. A citizen must obey health regulations —regardless of his conscience. A collective decision has been made that these activities promote an overriding common good, and dissent carried to the point of refusal is not permitted.

Of course, Selective Service involves a hazard that goes beyond anything previously described. But it also goes beyond any obligation that has been previously described. The objective is the defense of our country and the survival of our freedoms. And if we find ourselves embroiled in a conflict that does not truly fit that description, then our problem is to correct the errors that led to that situation—not to change the machinery that enables us to fight as a nation.

The pacifist is not confronted with any intellectual dilemma. He is responding to what he regards as a categorical imperative which forbids him to participate in killing under any circumstances and regardless of the consequences of his refusal. His premises may be wrong (and certainly are not accepted by a very large part of our population) but they involve no moral inconsistencies.

The outright opponent of a particular war is similarly free of any internal contradictions. He may have to indulge in mental gymnastics to prove that one war is moral and another immoral. His path may lead him to martyrdom (certainly it is hazardous). But he does not fall into the trap of approving the performance by others of what he regards as an immoral act and does not want to do himself.

Since those who advocate the volunteer army in the pure sense are willing to let others do the fighting, it is hard to avoid the feeling that they regard the word "immoral" as synonymous with "distasteful" rather than as an act which they will neither perform nor condone under any circumstances. Perhaps the individual elements of the English language require redefinition.

An interesting variation on the volunteer army concept is that of the "selective" conscientious objector. This thesis has few adherents. But it has attracted considerable attention because it lends itself to a type of argument which, though contrary to common sense and folk wisdom, has a tremendous impact upon anyone listening to it for the first time. This writer will never forget the moving eloquence of the late Father John Courtney Murray when he presented the case to his fellow members of the Burke Marshall Commission. It took considerable study, thought, and soul-searching to reject his recommendations on behalf of the majority.

The argument rests upon a proposal to extend the provisions of the Selective Service Act relating to conscientious objectors—provisions which have worked well and have encountered surprisingly little popular dissent even in World War II. In essence, the law permits the assignment to noncombatant military duty or to certain types of civilian work of those who sincerely believe that God has forbidden them to take part in any war. This concept has been broadened by a Supreme Court decision to cover those who are not members of a recognized religious denomination but who believe they are responding to an imperative command against military conflict from a universal force "parallel" in their lives to a belief in an orthodox Deity. The theology upon which this decision rested is abstruse but quite respectable. It flows from the late Paul Tillich, who thought that under some circumstances an atheist, whatever his words, could be a truly religious man, and a regular churchgoer, whatever his professions, could fail to believe in God.

The "selective" conscientious objector claims the same rights in rejecting participation in a particular war that the orthodox conscientious objector exercises in all wars. He buttresses his claim with the indisputable assertion that he is just as "sincere" as his more traditional counterpart. His conscience is as badly bruised if he is forced to bear arms in an "immoral" conflict as that of a pacifist in any conflict.

It is not very difficult to understand the practical problem standing in the way of enactment of the selective-objection concept even should legislators care to do so. If there were very many objectors, it would be impossible for any military commander to rely on his unit as a combat organization. He could not function if key members of his fighting team felt impelled on the eve of hostilities to debate the morality or immorality of the action. This issue must be settled in advance of his training and his assignment to a combat-ready post. The unlikelihood that such debates would take place on a large scale does not justify writing such a law.

The pacifist does not present the nation with this problem. It is known in advance that he is opposed to any form of slaughter. His reactions are predictable. His assignment—whether noncombatant military or civilian—can take these reactions into account. And it really does not matter to the law or the Defense establishment whether his religious beliefs are orthodox or otherwise. It is not enough, however, to answer what is considered to be a moral point by citing an *operational practicality*. It is therefore worthwhile to take

120

a closer look at the question of "sincerity" upon which the selective objector bases his case.

The first thought which arises is that sincerity in the draft law is merely a test by which it can be determined whether people do or do not fall under statutory provisions. It is not a quality which is either rewarded or punished solely for its own sake.

The pacifist is exempted from combat service because he is a pacifist—not because he is conscientious. His sincerity enters into the case only when a draft board or an appeals board is attempting to determine whether he really is what he says he is and not just a draft dodger trying to avoid an obligation to his country.

The point becomes clearer when the "selective" theory is tested against other, less emotion-laden, statutes. Our income-tax laws are tempered by many exemptions—for children, for charity, for elderly people, for the blind, for medical expenses. But no one has yet proposed an exemption for those who object sincerely to the manner in which the government spends its money. There are such individuals and some of them have refused to pay taxes because of their feelings. The theory is considered so ridiculous that the government generally does not even bother to prosecute but merely takes the money out of their bank accounts.

The more subtle and basic point, however, is the position of the selective objector vis-à-vis the society in which he lives. This position is different from that of the pacifist who is not objecting to a specific decision

121

by his country but to a general activity of humanity in which he has decided not to participate. His fellow countrymen have examined his position and, whether for good or bad reasons, have decided in advance to honor his decision under mutually agreed upon conditions. The question of the morality or immorality of a future decision does not arise. The pacifist will live in the same manner regardless of what happens.

The selective objector, on the other hand, is asking for the *protected* right of refusing to comply with a critical social decision *after it is made*. He is not seeking to protect the right to dissent (something which may need observance but not additional law) but a license to withdraw from his fellow countrymen in what they regard as a struggle for their survival.

It is here that the real moral question arises. The selective conscientious objector is asking for a contract with society in which he will stand back and permit the citizens of his country to fight an "immoral" war so long as they do not disturb him. To do so, he must make a deal. He must agree to refrain from obstructing immorality (or what he regards as immorality) in return for a promise that his life will not be made too uncomfortable. If this is morality, our dictionaries need rewriting.

The fact that the objector may be correct in his appraisal of *the* war as immoral does not alter his position. It merely undermines his request to be assigned work of national importance as an alternative to military duty. Any work that he performs will help the war effort. And logically, if he takes the word "immoral" seriously he has an obligation to hinder that effort by any device available to him. He cannot justify noncombatant service on the pacifist theory that war is always an aberration on the part of both sides and that therefore an honorable man is justified in ameliorating the suffering.

If a nation is acting immorally, an honorable man may be justified in resisting to the point of martyrdom. But he cannot expect his fellow citizens to agree with him or to provide him a cross without nails and a crown without thorns.

The real issue is whether war is justified under some circumstances. The majority of our citizens will agree that it is. Even though that majority can be wrong, it is within its power to take the steps that are regarded as necessary to prepare for combat. And once that stage is reached, the real moral issue is whether the burdens and the dangers shall fall upon all our citizens or be relegated to a minority.

It is useless to devise schemes based upon the assumption that the business of fighting is a profession like law, medicine, or journalism. The soldiers who maintain our military structure in peacetime are practicing a profession. They have what is socially regarded as an honorable career and can measure their service in terms of pay, allowances, and retirement. But war is

123

a question of survival, and this is in a different category altogether.

The issues are obscured by the fact that the nation is now engaged in an unpopular war. Eventually, like all human activities, the war will come to an end and, hopefully, life will return to normal. The volunteer-army debate will probably be forgotten, just as it was ignored in the late 1950's and early 1960's. Our military system will probably continue as it is now—based upon professional soldiers augmented by draftees when needed.

Individual viewpoints on morality will probably have very little to do with the ultimate decisions on military manpower. The men who must pass judgment are not immoral but are necessarily preoccupied with practical reactions to the environment. But this writer does not believe that the morality is on the side of "voluntarism" and immorality on the side of the draft. A good argument can be made for the opposite point of view.

The genuine moral issue, to anyone who agrees that a country can be justified in fighting a war, is whether it will act as a nation or a hedonistic society relying for its defense upon hired help. It acts as a nation only when its people share the burdens or at least share the hazards.

In the modern world, Selective Service is the only device thus far advanced which permits a complex, industrial economy to wage war effectively as a nation. There is no other way of allocating manpower for the combined social, economic, and military effort required by combat. Individual citizens cannot settle by negotiation or consensus the intricate questions of who will go to the infantry and who will go to the production line, who will be a machine gunner and who will be a riveter. These are decisions that cannot be voted upon once hostilities start. They can, however, be made under democratic procedures *if those procedures are determined by democratic methods in advance of the need for their use.*

It is this factor which gives Selective Service a value that goes far beyond its effectiveness as an organizing mechanism. It is probably the only way in which a democratic society can practice the undemocratic arts of warfare and still retain its freedoms.

A nation that goes to war *will* sharply curtail the normal options of life open to its citizens. This is one of the inevitabilities of modern society which will not be exorcized by incantations that recall Indian fighting on a frontier that vanished in the last century. The curtailments will not be submitted to a vote, except in a *pro forma* sense, after a nation has reached the conclusion that its survival is at stake.

Therefore, instead of hand wringing, it is prudent for those who value democracy to press in advance for procedures that will distribute the burdens equally during the fighting *and restore the normal options after it is over.*

Questions of cost and efficiency aside, the proposals

for the professional army in war as well as in peace do not meet this test. They assume that the burdens need NOT be equitably distributed but can be made a matter of choice. And in actuality, this would mean that the fighting would be left to the poor and the blacks who, for economic reasons, really have no choice.

The purpose of this essay is to focus attention on the pressing need to prepare ourselves for a true citizens' army when we must fight. A democracy involves obligations as well as privileges, and in no area of human endeavor is this principle more vital than when a society is facing the test of survival. To hire people to perform our obligations is the first step in the surrender of freedom.

There are larger questions before our nation—questions of our foreign policy and the responsiveness of our leadership to the popular will. These are beyond the scope of this book. The question here is how we will fight and who will do our fighting for us when everything else breaks down. Let us do it as a nation with all of our citizens involved.

About the Author

George E. Reedy served in the Johnson Administration as Special Assistant to the President. He was also a member of the President's National Advisory Commission on Selective Service. Mr. Reedy's distinguished career has also included the following positions: Press Secretary to President Johnson; Executive Director of the Senate Democratic Policy Committee (1953–1960); Senate correspondent for the United Press (1949–1951); United Press correspondent for the House of Representatives (1946–1949). He has also served on mediation boards in the settlement of various labor-management disputes. Presently Mr. Reedy is a lecturer and consultant on labor-management relations, oceanography, and public affairs, and has three books in progress.